Women Empowerment through Enterprise

Women Empowerment through Enterprise

Editors

Dr. Sanjeev Chaturvedi

Dr. Dibyendu Choudhury

Dr. Shreekant Sharma

GYAN

ni-msme

ISBN: 9788121214308

First Published, 2019

Published by

Gyan Publishing House
5, Ansari Road
Daryaganj, New Delhi-110002
Phone: 9811692060
E-mail: books@gyanbooks.com

and

National Institute for Micro, Small and Medium Enterprises (ni-msme)
(An Organisation of the Ministry of MSME, Govt. of India)
Yousufguda, Hyderabad-500045,
Telangana, India

Printed at: G. Print Process, Delhi.

Contents

Preface

We salute and celebrate women power, Udyam Sakhi is a network for nurturing social entrepreneurship creating business models revolving around low-cost products and services to resolve social inequities.

Shri Giriraj Singh
(Minister of State, Independent Charge)
Ministry of Micro, Small & Medium Enterprises, GoI

Women play a vital role in developing their family in all aspects - like development of children, support to her husband, development of her home, better society and better livelihood. The achievement of human development is dependent on the development and empowerment of women. Women entrepreneurship leads to women empowerment and it leads then to nation building.

The development and growth of a nation would not be possible unless women are brought into the mainstream of national development. As per the 2011 census women constitute about 48.5 percent of the total population in our country.

Entrepreneurship is the cure of many economy related problems as suggested by various researchers especially in developing nations like India. It specifically depends on the focus and commitment of the entrepreneur towards their venture. In the present time women are an emerging economic force. Social and economic development of women is necessary for the development of any country. Women entrepreneurship development initiatives, has helped in developing positive self-esteem as they gained self-confidence and were independent in making their own decisions, thereby reducing their dependence on their spouse/family members. The income from business had not only made the respondents financially strong, but made them decision makers. In early days woman wanted to start her own business but cannot succeed in the Indian environment due to male domination in the family and in society. Due to changing environment, men are now easily accepting women in entrepreneurial opportunity. The expanding service sector, production sector, central and state government policies are promoting woman entrepreneurship. But their activities are confined to limited areas and they are the victims of social prejudices and discrimination. This restricts the development of innovativeness, motivation, risk taking ability, etc., among women which are essential for entrepreneurial development. Women owned businesses are increasing in almost all the countries. The hidden entrepreneurial potentials of women has been gradually changing with the growing sensitivity to their role and economic status in the society. Improvement in skill, knowledge and adaptability in business are the main reasons for women entering into business ventures. Empowering woman entrepreneurs is essential for achieving the goals of sustainable development. Financial literacy among the rural women has been identified as one of the key competencies required for establishing, managing and thriving of the enterprise.

Government of India has taken up many initiatives like Stand-up India programme, which refers to promotion of micro, small and medium enterprises (MSMEs) by women and SC/ST entrepreneurs across the country with focus on rural, semi-urban areas, remote and less developed regions. In such programmes, the key players that deserve special mention are Ministry of MSME, Ministry of Skill Development and Entrepreneurship, Department of Science and Technology (DST), Ministry of Women & Child Development, Ministry of Minority Affairs, Bharatiya Mahila Bank (BMB), Small Industries Development Bank of India (SIDBI) etc.

Women have reached new frontiers in business and industry, bringing fresh ideas into the commercial and tech landscape of the world. The hidden entrepreneurial potentials of women have gradually been changing with the growing sensitivity to their role and economic status in the society. The role of woman entrepreneurs in the process of economic development has been recognised from the 1990s in various parts of the world. Today, in the world of business, woman entrepreneurship has become essential in many countries and has been accepted in all areas of work. Empowering woman entrepreneurs is essential for achieving the goals of sustainable development.

Women entrepreneurship can make a strong contribution to the economic well-being of the family and community. Highly educated, technically sound and professionally qualified women should be encouraged to manage their own business. Women entrepreneur networks are major sources of knowledge regarding entrepreneurship among women and they are increasingly recognised as a valuable tool for development and promotion of women entrepreneurs, particularly in poverty reduction and women empowerment, thus contributing to the Millennium Development Goals (MDGs). Full participation of women as entrepreneurs in all kinds of suitable businesses should therefore be encouraged. As promoting woman entrepreneurship is a sure path to rapid economic growth and development.

Over the years brilliant research papers have been published in the Sedme Journal, which find equal or even more relevance in the present times. On the occasion of Women Day, the ni-msme is bringing out this special edition containing selected research works on "Women Entrepreneurship" published in Sedme during 2000-2017. This book would be useful for entrepreneurs, researchers, policy makers & academicians.

Best Wishes

Editors

Dr. Sanjeev Chaturvedi

Dr. Dibyendu Choudhury

Dr. Shreekant Sharma

List of Contributors

1. **Dr. R. Supriya,** Assistant Professor and Research Scholar, Department of Commerce and Management, Sri Basaveshwara Govt. First Grade College, Mayakonda, Davangere District, Karnataka.
2. **Dr. Laxman P.** Associate Professor, Department of Studies in Commerce, Davangere University, Davangere-577004.
3. **Dr. Saif Siddiqui,** Assistant Professor, Centre for Management Studies, Jamia Millia Islamia – A Central University, Jamia Nagar, New Delhi-110025.
4. **Ms. Sumaira Jan,** Senior Research Fellow, Centre for Management Studies, Jamia Millia Islamia – A Central University, Jamia Nagar, New Delhi-110025.
5. **Dr. A. Selvakumar,** Research Scholar, Department of Economics, Bharathidasan University, Tiruchirappalli-23.
6. **Dr. P. Jayakumar,** Assistant Professor, Department of Economics, Government Arts College, Ariyalur.
7. **Dr. J.A. Arul Chellakumar,** Professor and Head, Department of Economics, Bharathidasan University, Khajamalai Campus, Tiruchirappalli – 23, Tamil Nadu.
8. **Dr. Narendra Jena,** Ph.D scholar at the Centre for the Study of Regional Development (CSRD), School of Social Sciences (SSS), Brahmaputra Hostel, R.N. 103 (Old), Jawaharlal Nehru University (JNU), New Delhi - 110 067
9. **Dr. Anil Kumar,** Professor, Haryana School of Business, Guru Jambeshwar University of Science & Technology, Hisar-125001 (Haryana)

10. **Dr. Parul,** Haryana School of Business, Guru Jambeshwar University of Science & Technology, Hisar-125001 (Haryana)
11. **Ms. Rodi Lalremruati**, Research Scholar, Department of Commerce, Mizoram University, Aizawl
12. **Dr. Rama Ramswamy,** Assistant Professor, Department of Commerce, Mizoram University, Aizawl
13. **Ms. Heena Saudagar,** Research Scholar-Department of Economics, Aligarh Muslim University, Aligarh, Uttar Pradesh-202001.
14. **Mr. Zeeshan,** Research Scholar, Department of Economics of Finance, New Academic Building (NAB), Birla Institute of Technology and Science (BITS), Pilani, Pilani Campus, District: Jhunjhunu , State: Rajasthan, Pincode: 333031.
15. **Dr. Shreekant Sharma,** Associate Faculty, School of Entrepreneurship and Extension, ni-msme, Yousufguda, Hyderabad - 500045.
16. **Dr. Krishnaveni Motha,** Assistant Zonal Manager, National Scheduled Tribes Finance and Development Corporation (NSTFDC) Zonal Office, 4th Floor, DSS Bhavan, Masab Tank, Hyderabad-500028.
17. **Mr. Bhabani Shankar Dash,** Research Scholar, P. G. Department of Business Management, Fakir Mohan University, Balasore.
18. **Dr. Bhagaban Das,** Professor, Head and Dean, P. G. Department of Business Management, Fakir Mohan University, Balasore.
19. **Dr. Soumendra Kumar Patra,** Associate Professor (OM & Decision Science), Ravenshaw University.
20. **Dr. Durga Madhab Mahapatra,** Lecturer and Head in Department of Commerce, MPC Autonomous College, Mayurbhanj, Odisha.
21. **Mrs. Seema Ghosh,** Assistant Professor, Bhavan's Vivekananda College, Sainikpuri, Hyderabad/Research Scholar, Osmania University, Hyderabad.

1

The Woman Entrepreneur - An Insight

R. Supriya
P. Laxmana

Abstract

Women owned businesses are increasing in almost all the countries. The hidden entrepreneurial potentials of women have gradually been changing with the growing sensitivity to their role and economic status in the society. Skill, knowledge and adaptability in business are the main reasons for women entering into business ventures.

Independence brought promise of equality of opportunity in all spheres to the Indian women and laws guaranteeing for their equal rights of participation in political process, and equal opportunities and rights in education and employment have been enacted. But, unfortunately, the government sponsored development activities have benefited only a small section of women in the urban middle class. A large majority of them are still unaffected by change.

The role of woman entrepreneurs in the process of economic development has been recognised from the 1990s in various parts of the world. Today, in the world of business, woman entrepreneurship has become essential in many countries and has been accepted in all areas of work.

Empowering woman entrepreneurs is essential for achieving the goals of sustainable development. The bottlenecks hindering their growth must be removed. Full participation of women as entrepreneurs in all kinds of suitable businesses should be encouraged. Proper training programmes should be initiated. Mentoring, newsletters, trade fairs / exhibitions can be a useful source of entrepreneurial development. Promoting woman entrepreneurship is a sure path to rapid economic growth and development.

Introduction

Woman owned businesses are highly increasing in the economies of almost all the countries. The hidden entrepreneurial potentials of women have gradually been changing with the growing sensitivity to their role and economic status in the society. Skill, knowledge and adaptability in business are the main reasons for women entering into business ventures. "Woman Entrepreneur" is a person who accepts a challenging role to meet her personal needs and become economically independent. A strong desire to do something positive is an in-built quality of entrepreneurial women, who are capable of contributing values to both family and the social life. With the advent of media, women are becoming aware of their own traits, rights and also the work situations. The glass ceilings are shattered and women are found indulging in every line of business from pappad to power cables. The challenges and opportunities provided to the woman of digital era are growing so rapidly that the job-seekers are turning into job-creators. They are flourishing as designers, interior decorators, exporters, publishers, garment manufacturers and are still exploring new avenues of economic participation. In India, although women constitute the majority of the total population, the entrepreneurial world is still male dominated. Women in advanced nations are recognised and are more prominent in the business world.

Independence brought the promise of equal opportunity in all spheres to the Indian women and laws guaranteeing for their equal rights of participation in political process and equal opportunities and rights in education and employment have been enacted. But, unfortunately, the government sponsored development activities have benefitted only a small section of women. The large majority of them are still unaffected by change and development activities have benefitted only a small percentage of women in the urban middle class.

The major challenges most of the developing countries and specially India is facing now are

- Jobless economic growth
- Problem of maximum utilisation of productive human resources, which is not possible if women are not provided

with right opportunity to build up their status in the society. One solution to both the above problems is to devise methods to encourage first generation entrepreneurs, which means we job providers need to be encouraged more rather than job seekers.

Economic independence will bring confidence among women, which will further bring about an awareness of their rights and privileges. For the prosperity of the nation it is important for the women to be educated, self-supporting and have positive self-image. Besides providing them with job opportunities one of the best ways to make them socially and economically independent is by effectively generating self-employment opportunities among them in their own areas. Entrepreneurship is a Herculean task fraught with struggle, entailing both risk and effort. No one can truly understand the triumphs, trials and tribulations of an entrepreneur other t han the person involved. While women have to go through the same stages of setting up an enterprise as do men, and have to face similar challenges, irrespective of gender, women do have a distinct set of factors that first impede their entry as entrepreneurs, and later their survival as successful business- women.

There are more than 100 lakh businesses owned by women, employing more than 130 lakh people and generating USD $1.9 trillion in sales. Not only that, women-led businesses are one of the fastest growing types of the small businesses—a rare bright spot in today's sluggish economy. The number of women-owned businesses increased by nearly 60 per cent since 1997. Lastly, according to the National Association of Women Business Owner's' (NAWBO) 2013 State of Women-Owned Businesses Survey, 2013 was to be the "Year of the Female Entrepreneur", with women business owners'optimism at high levels (81%) on the opportunities lying ahead.

Reasons for boosting women entrepreneurship

The role of women entrepreneurs in the process of economic development has been recognised from 1990s in various parts of the world. Today, in the world of business, women entrepreneurship has become an essential movement in many countries and has been accepted in all areas of working. The United Nations report has also concluded that economic development is closely related to the advancement of women. In nations where women have advanced, economic growth has usually been steady. By contrast, in countries where women have been restricted, the economy has been stagnant.

How to develop woman entrepreneurs

Right efforts from all quarters are required in the development of woman entrepreneurs and their greater participation in the entrepreneurial activities. Following efforts can be taken into account for effective development of woman entrepreneurs.

1. Women should be considered as specific target group for all developmental programmes.
2. Better educational facilities and schemes should be extended to women folk by the government.
3. Adequate training in management skills may be provided to women's community.
4. Women's participation in decision-making should be encouraged.
5. Vocational training needs to be extended to women's community to enable them to understand the production process and production management.
6. Skill development should be undertaken in women's polytechnics and industrial training institutes. Skills are put to work in training-cum-production workshops.
7. Training on professional competence and leadership skills must be extended to woman entrepreneurs.
8. Training and counselling should be arranged on a large scale for the existing woman entrepreneurs to remove psychological causes like lack of self-confidence and fear of success.
9. Counselling through the aid of committed NGOs, psychologists, managerial experts and technical personnel should be provided to existing and emerging woman entrepreneurs.

10. Continuous monitoring and improvement of training programmes is necessary.
11. Activities in which women are trained should focus on marketability and profitability.
12. Making provision for marketing and sales assistance from the government.
13. To encourage more passive woman entrepreneurs the women's training programmes should be organised that teach to recognise her own psychological needs and express them.
14. State finance corporations and financing institutions should be permitted by statute to extend purely trade related finance to woman entrepreneurs.
15. Women's development corporations have to gain access to open-ended financing.
16. The financial institutions should provide more working capital assistance both for small scale ventures and large scale ventures.
17. Provision of micro credit system and enterprise credit system should be made for woman entrepreneurs at local level.
18. Repeated gender sensitisation programmes should be held to train financiers to treat women with dignity and respect as persons in their own right.
19. Infrastructure, in the form of industrial plots and sheds, to set up industries is to be provided by state-run agencies.
20. Industrial estates could also provide marketing outlets for the display and sale of products made by women.
21. A Woman Entrepreneur's Guidance Cell may be set up to handle the various problems of woman entrepreneurs all over the state.
22. District Industries Centres and Single Window Agencies should be made use of for assisting women in their trade and business guidance.
23. Programmes for encouraging entrepreneurship among women are to be extended at local level.

24. Training in entrepreneurial attitudes should start at the high school level through well-designed courses, which build confidence through behavioural games.
25. More governmental schemes should be launched to motivate woman entrepreneurs to engage in small scale and large scale business ventures.
26. Involvement of non-governmental organisations in women's entrepreneurial training programmes and counseling is necessary.

Pull and push factors in making woman an entrepreneur

Entrepreneurship is a dynamic, risk taking activity which involves the way people think and live. It may start with some good idea or simply by finding a gap between the existing state and the ideal state of the market. Woman entrepreneurs are growing rapidly around the globe. The percentage is increasing every year. However, there are many factors leading women towards entrepreneurship. These factors could be classified into two basic categories: pull and push factors.

Here are some pull factors leading to entrepreneurship in women. Self-determination is the most important factor which leads to this dynamic activity. If any woman is determined to stand on her own, has desire to accept challenges and can withstand the problems she could possibly face in a male dominating world, she surely is a successful entrepreneur. However, many researches have shown that family support, and division and acceptability of household responsibilities between the spouses, is one conditional factor that can make woman an entrepreneur. Personal growth, learning and adventurous attitude, inner strength and self-achievement are all fruitful pull factors that take a woman into the world of entrepreneurs.

Many women prefer to be entrepreneurs because of the flexible work timings, as in routine 9 a.m. to 5 p.m. working hours, a woman may face job stress, negative job commitment and mental burn out. So, in order to avoid this situation they may take a step to start up their own businesses. Researches have also shown that entrepreneurial drive is also an important pull factor not only to make a woman an entrepreneur by title but also by achievement. Some women desire to attain social status and independence, hence they choose this path. Women with creative minds want to bring about change or come into entrepreneurial world with the objective of making a difference. Influential role models and successful business persons in the family are the factors that pull the woman towards entrepreneurship. These are main pull factors that lead a woman to entrepreneurship. However, these factors are normally seen in the developed countries of America, Europe, Australia and in some parts of Asia, such as China and Japan.

In under-developed and developing countries, the woman who faces a number of social and economic problems may not be pulled towards entrepreneurship because of the drive. They are being pushed by the circumstances to start up businesses. It is seen that many working women have to quit their jobs and win bread by entrepreneurial means. Failure to maintain work-life balance, gender inequality, threats and cases of harassment, stressful working hours may force the women to leave their jobs and start as entrepreneurs.

In many organisations women in equal posts with men are being under-paid, which causes frustration and job dissatisfaction. Glass ceiling and glass wall effect which do not allow women to expand in career are the root cause. Moreover, exclusion from networking in many offices lets women make such decisions. Other factors may be: less access to relevant training, stereotyping, difficulty in finding jobs, organisation politics and hostilities. Frequent lay-offs during the period of recession are also the push factors that make woman an entrepreneur.

Poverty and insufficient family income are also the factors that compel women to come into markets and start their own businesses. Frustration, conflict with management in offices or bad terms with life partner may also make woman an entrepreneur. In UDCs women are less educated, so they fail to find a respectable job. Furthermore, inflation and difficulty in running the house by being the sole bread earner can let woman to get herself engaged in entrepreneurial activities. Many women start their own businesses when the earner of their family is deceased. They have to support rest of the family. Unwilling natural succession may lead to entrepreneurship but this is very rare and is seen only in a few families of upper class.

Conclusion

Empowering woman entrepreneurs is essential for achieving the goals of sustainable development. The bottlenecks hindering their growth must be eradicated. Full participation of women as entrepreneurs in all kinds of suitable businesses should be encouraged. Proper training programmes should be initiated. Mentoring, newsletters, trade fairs / exhibitions can be a useful source of entrepreneurial-development. Promoting woman entrepreneurship is certainly a sure path to rapid economic growth and development.

Promoting entrepreneurship among women is certainly a short-cut to rapid economic growth and development. Let us try to eliminate all forms of gender discrimination and thus allow woman to be an entrepreneur at par with men. Every woman should take the time to think about what inspires her. Does each morning waker her up eager to get started? If not, it might be time for them to re-analyse the career choices. If they feel stuckup, they should tap into a broader community of women who are smart, savvy and successful. These women can help others breakthrough to the next level in their business so they too can be a part of the rise of woman entrepreneurs.

For hundreds, even thousands of years, women have been successful entrepreneurs. Their unique mindset, viewpoints, attitudes and skills as women have all contributed to their successes in business.

2

Determinants of Entrepreneurial Intensity Among Woman Entrepreneurs: Evidence from Jammu & Kashmir

Saif Siddiqui
Sumaira Jan

Abstract

Entrepreneurship is the cure of many economy related problems as suggested by various researchers especially in developing nations like India. It specifically depends on the focus and commitment of the entrepreneur towards their venture, measuring their level of entrepreneurial intensity. This intensity, if high, can lead to greater organisational growth, societal benefits, etc. In Indian states like Jammu & Kashmir, where low GDP and high unemployment are major challenges, higher entrepreneurial intensity can prove to be a stepping stone. What role woman entrepreneurs can play in it is being continuously assessed by researchers on a growing scale. The present study assesses the level of intensity among the woman entrepreneurs of Jammu & Kashmir and suggests some measures to enhance the same. The results reveal that there is low entrepreneurial intensity among woman entrepreneurs of the state in terms of their innovativeness, risk-taking and autonomy.

Keywords: *entrepreneurial intensity, woman entrepreneurs, Jammu & Kashmir*

Introduction

Entrepreneurship is universally recognised as an effective instrument of economic development for any country, be that developed or developing. In India entrepreneurship was previously seen in light of its culture, customs, and so on, but now the trend has changed and it is believed that for the success of any entrepreneur their vision, innovativeness and risk-taking ability will play the key role. Researchers like Shaver and Scott (1991) and Low and Macmillan (1988) have explained certain characteristics which differentiate entrepreneurs from the commoners including ambition, need for achievement, risk taking, and locus of control. Entrepreneurs have something in them which differentiates them from the rest. This something is an inner drive to do and be different. Most commonly this inner drive is explained as an entrepreneurial intensity.

Entrepreneurial intensity (EI) measures the level of focus and commitment of an entrepreneur towards his/her venture. Several models of entrepreneurial intensity have been proposed by researchers. Some say that it significantly impacts the venture performance, some establish that it creates sustainable advantage for the individuals, organisations and societies, while others believe that it helps formulating high growth strategies for businesses.

Entrepreneurship is now recognised as a vehicle for providing equal opportunities to men and women in India. Shah (2012) believes that, for economic growth in India, more woman entrepreneurs should be generated as they can return 90 per cent of every unit of investment made on them. As per Nelasco (2008), women in India have high leadership potential but it is significantly lowered by their socio-economic and political restrictions. In such a scenario, emerging as successful entrepreneurs will require them to be extra-ordinarily motivated and have high entrepreneurial intensity, which will differentiate them from the rest.

The state of Jammu & Kashmir (J & K) in India belongs to the northern part and is different in terms of its demographic profile, societal norms, culture and trading. Parihar et al. (2013) conducted a study in the state of Jammu & Kashmir which reveals that woman entrepreneurs have low entrepreneurial competencies/intensity and face numerous problems. It is known from the annual report of the Ministry of Statistics and Programme Implementation, Government of India, that the annual GDP of Jammu & Kashmir in 2014-15 was INR 87, 92, 100 lakh, which is one of the lowest in India. Its unemployment rate as per the fourth Annual Employment Unemployment Survey (2013-14) report by the Ministry of Labour and Employment, Government of India was 4.9 per cent, which is one of the highest in the country.

Combining these two aspects and the fact that entrepreneurship can be a great source of enhancing GDP and reducing unemployment, this study proposes to enhance core entrepreneurial competencies among woman entrepreneurs of the state by empirically investigating the status of various entrepreneurial traits including innovativeness, pro-activeness, risk-taking and autonomy. A training model can be provided for the same which will eventually enhance the level of woman entrepreneurship in the state which will have a direct influence on the overall GDP and employment status of the state.

Literature review

Srivastava and Misra (2017) in their study propose that social valuation is an important determinant of entrepreneurial intention among women in India. Entrepreneurial education significantly influences the level of entrepreneurial intensity among women in the country as per this study. Langowitz and Minnit (2007) propose that entrepreneurship is becoming a very important source of employment for women across various nations, although the rate is lower than that of men. Based on a large sample of individuals in 17 countries and using behavioural economics approach, they tried to decipher the variables influencing the entrepreneurial propensity/intensity of women in those countries. Perceptual variables were also used in addition to certain demographic and economic variables. The results revealed that women tend to perceive entrepreneurial environment less favourably irrespective of their level of motivation in the sample countries. Subjective perceptual variables were found to greatly influence the entrepreneurial intensity of women and account for much of the difference between entrepreneurship among men and women.

Urban and Sefalafala (2015) investigate the influence of entrepreneurial intensity and capabilities on the performance of the firm. Using a sample size of 117 firms with international presence, operating in South Africa, the research design used in this study was cross-sectional and quantitative. Using correlation and regression tools, the results of the study reveal that entrepreneurial intensity and capabilities are positively related with the performance of the firms. Environmental hostility was found to have a weak moderating effect on this relationship. The study suggests that firms should focus on enhancing their level of innovativeness, pro-activeness and risk-taking in order to ensure increased performance. Heibrunn (2008) conducted a study to explore the factors which influence entrepreneurial intensity among Kibbutz communities in Israel. The data was collected from 60 respondents using structured questionnaire. The concept of entrepreneurial grid is used by this study to explore community entrepreneurship. The results reveal that organisational age and size do have an impact on the level of entrepreneurial intensity. Morris and Sexton conducted a study in 1996 to determine the implications of entrepreneurial intensity on company. The region chosen for the study was Florida and the sample size was 210 industrial firms. Key dimensions considered by the study include: innovativeness, pro-activeness and risk-taking. The results revealed high level of relationship between entrepreneurial intensity and firm performance. This relationship becomes even stronger when emphasis is placed on the degree of entrepreneurship rather than on the extent of entrepreneurship.

Gundry and Welsch (2001) used a sample size of 832 woman entrepreneurs in USA to conduct a survey about their growth intentions along certain strategic dimensions. The results revealed that high growth oriented entrepreneurs are different from low-growth oriented entrepreneurs along several dimensions. High- growth oriented woman entrepreneurs had a much greater focus on new technologies and expansion of market which allowed them to exhibit higher levels of entrepreneurial intensity. This intensity was found to be very low in case of low growth oriented woman entrepreneurs. Scheepers et al. (2007) studied the levels of entrepreneurial intensity in South African firms. This study is based on a comparative analysis of Information and Communication Technology (ICT) companies with that of listed

Johannesburg Stock Exchange companies (excluding ICT listings). Using cross-sectional telephonic survey, the results reveal that ICT companies have higher levels of entrepreneurial intensity than those listed on the JSE. The size of the company revealed no relationship, while age was found to be negatively correlated with intensity. It means older the company, less entrepreneurially intense it becomes and vice-versa. Gundry et al. (2003) in their study explain the influence of certain factors on the growth and implementation of new technologies in women owned businesses. The study proposes that it is the growth of the market which mediates the relation between entrepreneurial intensity, opportunity costs and the technological change. New growth strategies in woman entrepreneurs are induced by their entrepreneurial intensity and willingness to incur opportunity costs as per this study.

Mustafa (2013) brought to light the prospects and challenges of woman entrepreneurship in the state of Jammu and Kashmir. This study was done by circulating a structured questionnaire among 60 woman entrepreneurs in different regions of the state. Support from government in the form of subsidies, incentives, etc., was seen to significantly motivate woman entrepreneurs. Irrespective of these problems, there are still a significant number of entrepreneurs in the state in all the three regions including Kashmir, Jammu and Ladakh. Shah and Mustafa (2014) in their study on woman entrepreneurship in the state of Jammu and Kashmir discuss that the state has a large number of unemployed women consisting of significant number of widows and half-widows. This calls for an overall economic development for ensuring the sovereignty of development in the state. Studies reveal a strong interaction between socio-economic status of women in the state and their entry into the work-force. This study was done by conducting a survey among 75 woman entrepreneurs of different parts of the Kashmir valley. The study revealed that although challenges are many in their way women are showing up in entrepreneurship at a good rate. The study reveals the inner drive of women, financial support, familial support, etc., to be among the numerous factors for motivating women to take up entrepreneurship. The government's policy towards providing subsidies and incentives tends to motivate women for entrepreneurship.

The review of literature revealed different dimensions of entrepreneurial intensity. Most important among them that have been used in the present study include: innovativeness, pro-activeness, risk-taking, competitive aggressiveness and autonomy.

Research gap

After the review of relevant literature it was found that most of the studies on entrepreneurial intensity were conducted in the developed nations where the economic and social conditions are quite different than the developing and the under developed ones. Studies on this topic were found to be rare with respect to women in India and highly scarce with respect Jammu and Kashmir. Using the concept of entrepreneurial intensity as a tool for economic development in terms of high GDP and low unemployment was found to be non-prevalent. So a research gap is quite evident.

Data and methodology

Research objectives

The study set out with the below stated research objectives.

1. To identify the contribution of various dimensions towards entrepreneurial intensity among woman entrepreneurs of the state of Jammu and Kashmir
2. To identify the dimensions of entrepreneurial intensity to be enhanced to improve the level of entrepreneurship among the woman entrepreneurs of the state
3. To develop a model depicting the contribution of various dimensions towards the overall entrepreneurial intensity in the state

Materials and methods

The data used in this study has been collected by administering a structured questionnaire among 450 woman entrepreneurs belonging to the state of J & K in India, out of whom 405 responded. Thus the present study is based on responses from 405 woman entrepreneurs. The primary survey was done during June 2016 to September 2016.

The entrepreneurs were randomly selected from the list provided by Jammu and Kashmir Entrepreneurship Development Institute situated in Srinagar. The respondents were asked questions about their entrepreneurial traits including innovativeness, pro-activeness, risk-taking, competitive aggressiveness and autonomy. These woman entrepreneurs were from different districts of the state including: Srinagar, Jammu, Budgam, Baramulla, Pulwama, Kulgam and Shopian.

Data analysis and interpretation

Before moving on with the empirical analysis the instrument used was checked for its reliability and validity using composite reliability. Hair et al., (2010) proposed that data is reliable when its composite reliability (CR) is greater than 0.7. In the current study, CR was found to be 0.936, 0.917, 0.918, 0.985 and 0.924 for risk-taking, innovativeness, pro-activeness, competitive aggressiveness and autonomy respectively. The validity was checked by presenting the scale to the experts in the field of entrepreneurship. Hence the scale used is both valid as well as reliable.

Confirmatory factor analysis (CFA)

Confirmatory factor analysis is a very important modelling technique which is used to map certain measures on to theoretical constructs. This is depicted by the loadings of the corresponding constructs. Using second order CFA in the current study will help ascertain if innovativeness, pro-activeness, competitive aggressiveness, risk-taking and autonomy load adequately on entrepreneurial intensity among woman entrepreneurs of the state of J & K.

For this purpose Mplus Version 7 was used developed by Muthen and Muthen (1998). After performing second order CFA, it was found that only two constructs (i.e., pro-activeness and competitive aggressiveness) out of five dimensions are significantly loading for woman entrepreneurs of J & K with values of 0.836 and 0.95 respectively. For innovativeness, risk-taking and autonomy the values were found to be 0.335, 0.415 and 0.134 respectively, thus making them insignificant for the current study. The details are presented in table-1.

Table - 1: Factor loadings of various items on their respective constructs

Factor (R^2)	*Items*	*Factor loadings*				
		I	*II*	*III*	*IV*	*V*
Innovativeness (11.2% of variance)-INN	Over the next few years we could change up to 50% of the processes that support our current business model (Inn1)	.894				
	We have already put measurable resources(human and financial) behind our innovation agenda (Inn2)	.861				
	We have a good record of rolling out new products and services in the market (Inn3)	.399				
	Innovation is a core value in this organisation (Inn4)	.45				
	Our strategic planning process is oriented towards grabbing the opportunity (Inn5)	.94				
	Our strategic initiatives aim at gaining competitive advantage (Inn6)	.914				
	We strongly emphasize research and development, technological leadership andinnovations (Inn7)	.885				
Pro-activeness (70% of variance)-PA	We believe in moving carefully, while ceasing opportunities in the market (PA1)		.571			
	In dealing with competition, we initiate actions which the competitors then respond to(PA2)		.984			
	In dealing with competitors, we prefer to adopt the live and let live strategy (PA3)		.87			
	Our firm is always the one to initiate strategies and bring new products/services in the market than the competitors (PA4)		.96			
Competitive aggressiveness (90.3% of variance)-CA	We are prepared to launch a new product/service even when it is unclear how successful it may be (CA1)			.978		
	We are aggressive and intensely competitive in taking business away from the competitors (CA2)			.974		
	We make every possible attempt to stay ahead of our competitors (CA3)			.983		

(*Contd...*)

Risk-taking (17.2% of variance)- RT	Problem is studied very thoroughly before deploying resources to solve it (RT1)				.891			
	High risk projects are preferred overlow risk projects in our firm (RT2)				.874			
	When faced with a decision making situation under uncertainty, we adopt a wait and see strategy (RT3)				.833			
	It is always good to study the environment properly before taking any decision in theorganisation (RT4)				.946			
Autono my (1.8% of variance)- AUT	We support the efforts of individuals/teams that work autonomously (AUT1)					.919		
	Individuals/teams take decisions on their own without consulting superiors (AUT2)					.755		
	Individuals/teams are expected to use out-of-the- box strategies in the pursuit of opportunities (AUT3)					.857		
	In my firm the top management decides which opportunities to pursue (AUT4)					.929		

Factor loadings of various items on their respective construct

The model fit indices are presented in table-2.

Table-2: Model diagnostics

Chi-square (÷2)	445.069
Degree of freedom (df)	204
P-Value	0.0000
Scaling correction factor for MLR	0.7577
CFI (Comparative fit index)	0.946
TLI (Tucker-Lewis index)	0.938
RMSEA(Root mean square error of approximation)	0.05
SRMR (Standard root mean square residual)	0.039

*significant at $P<0.01$

The model fit indices are all in their prescribed range and hence are supporting the model:

CFI- It should be greater than 0.9 for a model to be acceptable (Cheung & Rensvold, 2002).

TLI- Acceptable value for this index is 0.9 (Cheung & Rensvold, 2002).

RMSEA- Model is acceptable if value is less than or equal to 0.05 (Browne & Cudeck, 1993).

SRMR- Value below 0.80 is a good fit (Hu & Bentler, 1999).

x^2/df (Relative chi-square): It should preferably be less than 3 for a good model fit (Carmnines & Mclver, 1981).

Thus a good model fit has been achieved with respectable factor loadings, indicating an efficacious CFA. The model with all its loadings is presented at figure-1.

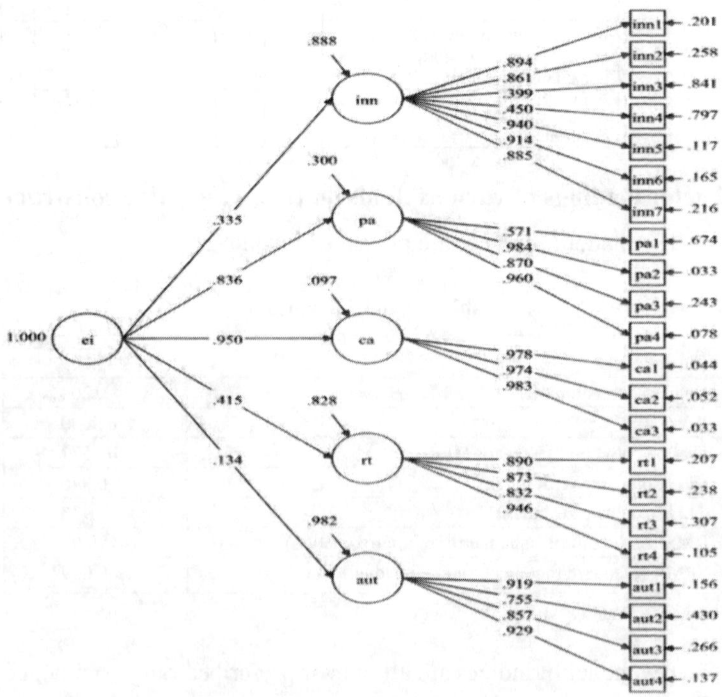

ei- entrepreneurial intensity; inn-innovativeness; rt-risk-taking; aut-autonomy; pa-pro activeness; ca- competitive aggressiveness)

Fig. 1: Model loadings

Table-1 shows that all the variables including innovativeness, pro-activeness, competitive aggressiveness, risk-taking and autonomy load significantly on entrepreneurial intensity among woman entrepreneurs of the state of Jammu and Kashmir, as the values are higher than .75 in almost all the cases. Some researchers suggest that even a loading of 0.4 is respectable, (Bowen & Guo 2011) but here they are considered only for the reason that good model fit has been achieved.

Results and discussion

The results of this study reveal that the scale used is both reliable and valid. It means that this scale can be used for further research in assessing entrepreneurial intensity among woman entrepreneurs of the state. The study also shows that innovativeness, pro-activeness, risk-taking, competitive aggressiveness and autonomy significantly load on entrepreneurial intensity among woman entrepreneurs of the state of Jammu and Kashmir. All of them show reasonable loadings which prompts such inference.

Further analysis of second order CFA reveal that out of the five dimensions used, only two, i.e., pro-activeness and competitive aggressiveness are significantly high among woman entrepreneurs of the state. The rest of the three - innovativeness, risk- taking and autonomy - are low. From this it can be deduced that woman entrepreneurs portray lower intensity on three among five dimensions of entrepreneurial intensity.

This study proposes that there is low level of entrepreneurial intensity among business women of the state of J & K. Training has to be provided to them to increase their level of innovativeness, risk-taking and autonomy. Once it increases, it will improve the overall level of entrepreneurship in the state which, in turn, will enhance the overall economic condition of the state. The direct and strong relationships between entrepreneurial intensity and entrepreneurship, and entrepreneurship and economic development have already been deduced by the numerous researchers.

Conclusion

The most important take-away of this study is that woman entrepreneurs of Jammu and Kashmir exhibit low entrepreneurial intensity on three constructs (innovativeness, risk-taking and autonomy) out of the five (innovativeness, risk- taking, pro-activeness, competitive aggressiveness and autonomy) considered for the study. It leads to the inference that woman entrepreneurs of the state are wanting in terms of being innovative, risk-taking and providing autonomy to people working in their organisations.

This study provides a scale which can be used for further research in the field of entrepreneurial intensity among woman entrepreneurs of Jammu and Kashmir.

3

Problems and Prospects of Women Entrepreneurs in Tamil Nadu with Special Reference to Pudukkottai District

A. Selvakumar
P. Jayakumar
J.A. Arul Chellakumar

Abstract

Women entrepreneurship has been recognised as an important source of economic growth. With the advent of media, women are aware of their own traits, rights and also the work situations. The glass ceilings are shattered and women are found involved in every line of business from pappad to power cables. Tamil Nadu has a strong micro, small and medium enterprises (MSME) base with nearly 7 lakh registered units, the highest for any state in India. Tamil Nadu is one of the most industrialised states in the country. In terms of contribution of the manufacturing sector to the net state domestic product, the state ranks next to Maharashtra. The study aims at examining the entrepreneurial development among women and relationship between the socio-economic backgrounds of women entrepreneurs, highlighting the motivational forces emanating from the District Industrial Centre and Mahalir Thittam in the Pudukkottai district. The paper talks about the status of women entrepreneurs and the problems faced by them when they had ventured out to carve their own niche in the competitive world of business environment.

Introduction

Women owned businesses are highly increasing in the economies of almost all countries. The hidden entrepreneurial potential in women have gradually been changing with the growing sensitivity to their role and economic status in the society. Skill, knowledge and adaptability in business are the main reasons for women to enter into business ventures. 'Woman entrepreneur'is a person who accepts a challenging role to meet her personal needs and become economically independent. A strong desire to do something positive is an in-built quality of entrepreneurial women, who are capable of contributing values in both family and social life. With the advent of media, women have become aware of their own traits, rights and also about the work situations. Glass ceilings have been shattered and women are now engaging in every line of business from pappad to power cables. Tamil Nadu has a strong MSME base with nearly 7 lakh registered units, the highest for any state in India. Tamil Nadu is one of the most industrialised states in the country. In terms of contribution of the manufacturing sector to the net state domestic product, the state ranks next to Maharashtra.

The challenges and opportunities provided to the women of digital era are growing so rapidly that the job seekers are turning into job creators. They are flourishing as designers, interior decorators, exporters, publishers, garment manufacturers and are exploring still newer avenues of economic participation. In India, although women constitute the majority of the total population, the entrepreneurial world is still a male dominated one. Women in advanced nations are recognised as business women and are more prominent in the business world. But the Indian women entrepreneurs are facing constraints like lack of access to formal finance mechanisms; limited mobility and access to information and networks. Hence, it was not easy for these women to succeed in business. They had to face a number of difficulties and overcome a number of barriers to become successful in their ventures. Moreover, they had to deal with discrimination and withstand skepticism by the society, and also put in more effort than men to prove their credibility to others.

Women entrepreneurs

Women Entrepreneurs may be defined as the women or a group of women who initiate, organise and operate a business enterprise.

The Government of India has defined women entrepreneurs as an enterprise owned and controlled by women having a minimum financial interest of 51 per cent of the capital and giving at least 51 per cent of the employment generated in the enterprise to women. Women entrepreneurs are engaged in business due to push and pull factors which encourage them to have an independent occupation and stands on their own legs. A sense towards independent decision-making on their life and career is the motivational factor behind this urge. Saddled with household chores and domestic responsibilitie women want independence. Influenced by these factors the women entrepreneurs choose this profession as a challenge and from an urge to do something new. Such a situation is described as pull factors. Push factors are those where women are engaged in business activities due to family compulsion and the responsibility is thrust upon them.

Objectives of the study

The following objectives are given below:

1. To study the socio-economic status of the women entrepreneurs in the study area
2. To analyse the problems of women entrepreneurs in running their enterprises in Pudukkottai district

Profile of the study area

The Pudukkottai district has been selected for this study as this district has potential for entrepreneurship. The district is endowed with several facilities for the conducive growth of women entrepreneurs as compared to other districts in Tamil Nadu. Hence it was felt that this district was ideally suited for a study on women entrepreneurship.

Mode of sample selection

Pudukkottai district has eleven taluks. In all the eleven taluks, the researcher has come across 230 women entrepreneurs who had been maintaining micro and small scale enterprises for more than three years. The details of the women entrepreneurs of the district were collected from the District Industries Centre (DIC) in Pudukkottai district. Thus all the 230 women entrepreneurs were selected for the study by using the census sampling. Out of 230 samples, 168 were micro entrepreneurs and 62 were small scale entrepreneurs.

Method of data collection and tools of analysis

Thus, the researcher has interviewed all the 230 women entrepreneurs for the purpose of the present study, which is based on both primary and secondary data. The primary data was collected by using a well structured interview schedule. The prepared interview schedule was characterised with open ended questionnaires. The tools of analysis consisted of simple percentages and contribution level of women entrepreneurs.

Economic assistance of women entrepreneurs

Magalir Thittam is the name for the upscaled Tamil Nadu Women's Development Project (TNWDP). This project is intended to promote economic development and social empowerment among poor women through a network of SHGs formed with the active support of NGOs and the bank-linkage programme.

Table - 1: Economic assistance to women entrepreneurs: block-wise detail Pudukkottai district (2010-11)

Sl. No.	*Name of the block*	*No. of micro enterprises*	*SC*	*MI*	*OC*	*Total*	*EA subsidy*	*Bank loan*	*Total*
1.	Annavasal	2	--	--	26	26	1.760	5.240	7.000
2.	Aranthangi	6	39	0	50	89	5.280	17.280	22.560
3.	Arimalam	12	42	19	142	203	10.560	35.320	45.880
4.	Avudaiyarkoil	24	166	84	115	365	21.120	73.910	95.030
5.	Manamelkudi	16	74	66	112	252	14.080	45.010	59.090
6.	Ponnamaravathi	8	0	41	75	116	7.040	41.740	48.780
7.	Thirumayam	7	34	21	38	93	6	27	33
8.	Viralimalai	8	54	0	53	107	7.040	18.380	25.420
9.	Karambakkudi	39	304	29	321	654	34.320	119.360	153.680
10.	Thiruvarankulam	100	475	440	593	1508	88.000	364.00	452.590
11.	Gandarvakottai	30	109	0	374	483	26.400	85.190	111.890

Source: Project Implementation Unit, Mahalir Thittam, Pudukkottai.

In Pudukkottai district, there are both large and small scale industries. The large scale industries are mainly engaged in the areas of textiles and chemicals. The small scale industries are engaged in wood work, tinkering, fabrication of metal products, printing and binding, manufacture of agricultural implements, manufacture of cement products, automobile servicing and repairing, and safety matches. In addition to small scale industries, there are also a number of village and cottage industries. Prominent among them are pottery, blacksmithy, carpentry, small lime kilns, small brick kilns, basket making rope making, and synthetic gem cutting.

Role of district industries centre

The Government is also in active move in promoting self-employment opportunity in urban and rural areas by extending financial assistance through banking sector for the establishment and development of micro and small enterprises. The District Industries Centre is the institution at the district level, which provides all the services and supports, facilitates the women entrepreneurs for setting up micro and small enterprises in Pudukkottai district. The District Industrial Centre, Pudukkottai has been pursuing the basic objectives by assisting for optimum utilisation in existing industries, faster promoting of micro, small and medium enterprises in rural and urban areas and by increasing the employment opportunities in industrial sector.

Table - 2: Scheme-wise contribution to employment by women MSEs of Pudukkottai district (2010-11)

Year	*Scheme*	*Total*	*Women*	*Employment*
2006-2007	PMRY	49	23	49
2007-2008	PMRY	95	42	55
2008-2009	PMEGP	22	8	46
2009-2010	PMEGP	44	14	47
2010-2011	PMEGP	48	16	110
2011-2012	UYEGP	41	9	53
Total		**299**	**113**	**360**

Source: Official records, DIC, Pudukkottai.

The micro and small entrepreneurs required and received various types of assistance under the new schemes of PMRY, PMEGP, and UYEGP of the District Industries Centre. Out of 299 units, 113 units were being run by the women entrepreneurs of the Pudukkottai district, and 360 women are contributing to employment opportunities in this region.

Entrepreneurship is an economic activity that functions in a socio-cultural setting. In order to find out the characteristics of women entrepreneurs who are increasingly assuming entrepreneurial activities, their socio-economic background has been studied. The below given table reiterates the socio-economic status of the women entrepreneurs of the Pudukkottai district.

It could be inferred from table -3 that majority of women entrepreneurs belonged to age category 41 to 50 (65.21%). The table also reveals that majority of 186 (80.87%) women entrepreneurs had completed their studies up to secondary level. It is also evident that 65.22 per cent of women entrepreneurs belonged to backward communities and 82.17 per cent of women entrepreneurs were married. Moreover, 38.70 per cent of women entrepreneurs were hailing from families with 5 or 6 members. Of the remaining, majority of 87 (37.83%) women entrepreneurs were earning an income of Rs. 10,000-15,000 per month.

Table - 3: Socio-economic Conditions of Women Entrepreneurs in Pudukkottai District

Sl. No	Agecategory	No. of respondents	Percentage
1.	25-35 yrs	15	6.52
	36-40 yrs	40	17.39
	41-45 yrs	55	23.91
	46-50 yrs	95	41.30
	51- 60 yrs	25	10.87
	Total	230	100.00
	Educational qualification	No. of respondents	Percentage
2.	Up to 10 level	103	44.78
	Higher secondary/diploma	83	36.09
	Degree	28	12.17
	PG/ professional	16	6.96
	Total	230	100.00

(Contd...)

	Community	No. of respondents	Percentage
3.	OC	20	8.70
	BC	150	65.22
	MBC	41	17.83
	SC/ST	19	8.26
	Total	230	100.00
	Marital status	No. of respondents	Percentage
4.	Unmarried	24	10.43
	Married	189	82.17
	Others (W/D/S)	17	7.39
	Total	230	100.00
	Family size	No. of respondents	Percentage
5.	1 or 2	40	17.39
	3 or 4	65	28.26
	5 or 6	89	38.70
	7 or 8	36	15.65
	Total	230	100.00
	Monthly income (in Rs.)	No. of respondents	Percentage
6.	4000 to 10000	68	29.57
	10000 to 15000	87	37.83
	15000 to 20000	40	17.39
	20000 to 25000	21	9.13
	25000 to 50000	14	6.09
	Total	230	100.00

Source: Compiled from primary data.

Nature of business

Micro and small enterprises have a major role in the country's economic development through their contribution to rural development and creation of employment opportunities for the women in Pudukkottai district. Women entrepreneurs have been operating majority of micro and small scale enterprises in this area. The micro and small scale enterprises face many difficulties and they need organisations specialised in providing support to female entrepreneurs.

Table - 4: Distribution of respondents based on nature of business

Sl.No	*Nature of business*	*Number of respondents*	*% of respondents*
1	Micro	168	73.04
2	Small	62	26.96
	Total	230	100.00

Source: Compiled from primary data.

They clearly feel that this is one area where their clients face greater difficulties than their male counterparts.

73.04 per cent of women entrepreneurs were performing micro level business activities; 26.96 per cent of women entrepreneurs were performing small level business activities. It could be inferred that the level of business activities performed by women entrepreneurs was low with micro enterprises units occupying 73.04 per cent. The reasons shall be lack of confidence to run bigger industrial units or inability to plan big or risk aversion mentality.

Problems of women entrepreneurs

Women entrepreneurs face many problems in their efforts for developing their enterprise. Being a woman itself poses various problems to a woman entrepreneur and therefore compared to men the problems of women entrepreneurs are numerous. The problems range from mobilising various resources including the problem of capital, marketing, raw material, sales, labour, technical, competition, new technology, problem of land/ shed/ water/ power/ taxes, lack of family support as well as lack of government support and the like.

Hence their problems arise both from within and from outside, and also differ from enterprise to enterprise. Some of these problems are similar to all, whereas some others are more specific and related to the line of activity of the enterprise. Some have the problem of external environment. Whatever be the problem, there is no prescribed formula to deal with them. The problems have to be dealt with by the entrepreneurs themselves; otherwise they would affect the working of the enterprise itself. Efficient and timely handling of the problems leads to the success of the enterprise.

Table - 5: Distribution of respondents based on major problems

Sl. No.	*Problems*	*Number of respondents*	*% of respondents*	*% contribution*
1.	Employees	110	47.83	13.19
2.	Working capital	92	40.00	11.03
3.	Poor Government support	67	29.13	8.03

(*Contd...*)

4	High cost for raw materials	43	18.70	5.16
5	Business competition	71	30.87	8.51
6	Poor marketing support	65	28.26	7.79
7	Poor bankers'support	59	25.65	7.07
8	Lack of support from suppliers	34	14.78	4.08
9	Lack of support from retailers	51	22.17	6.12
10	Inadequate finance	79	34.35	9.47
11	High interest	48	20.87	5.76
12	Lack of infrastructure	45	19.57	5.40
13	Quality problems	47	20.43	5.64
14	Inadequate power supply	23	10.00	2.76
	Total	834		100.00

Source: Compiled from primary data.

The above table shows that the following problems have been faced by the women entrepreneurs in Pudukkottai district:

- The notion of women in industry itself has to be defined and further sub-divided. It is not functionally enough to state that it means all enterprises run by women and are having more than 47.83 per cent of women employees. More important aspects are the background of the entrepreneur as also who are the entrepreneur and who her workers are.
- Another problem of women entrepreneurs is managing the working capital. Working capital is required for maintaining finished stock to meet the market demand, for production and meeting marketing and other administrative expenses. It will be very difficult for women entrepreneurs to avail such loan facilities from financial institutions as they are unable to provide security. Forty per cent of the women entrepreneurs were facing working capital problems in Pudukkottai district.
- Government support is a key element of every business activity. The Government of India established many developmental and promotional institutions for the promotion of micro enterprises for women, but 29.13 per cent of the women entrepreneurs to feel that government support is very poor in providing of information, training, providing funds and so on.

- They have to even face the problems of scarcity of raw materials and necessary inputs. On top of this, it is the high prices of raw materials, on one hand and getting raw materials at minimum discount rates on the other. 18.70 per cent of the women entrepreneurs feel that the raw material prices are high.
- Women entrepreneurs do not have a proper organisational set-up to pump in a lot of money for canvassing and advertisements. Thus they have to face a stiff competition with the men entrepreneurs who easily involve in the promotion and development, and carry out easy marketing of their products with both the organised sector and their female counterparts. Such a competition ultimately results in the liquidation of women entrepreneurs. 30.87 per cent of the women entrepreneurs were facing such stiff competition in their business.
- Women have to face a number of challenges in the market because of stiff competition. Many business women find it difficult to capture the market and compete with their product. Of the sample, 28.26 per cent of women entrepreneurs had considered 'poor marketing support' as a major problem.
- Women do not generally have property in their own names to use that as collateral security for obtaining loans/funds from banks and other financial institutions. Thus their access to external sources is very limited. Secondly, the banks also consider women less credit-worthy and discourage women borrowers by the belief that women cannot repay the amount of loans taken. Of the sample women entrepreneurs 25.65 per cent feel that bankers' support is very poor with respect to the start up of their enterprises.
- During the processing of products, women entrepreneurs faced many problems due to lack of support from suppliers viz. poor location of shop, lack of transport facility and tough competition from larger and established units. Among the sample, 14.78 per cent of women entrepreneurs had complained about lack of support from suppliers to process the products.

- Nearly half (22.17%) of the women entrepreneurs feel that lack of support from retailers which included businesses like purchase and sale of products with little or no processing, like provision stores, fancy stores.
- Finance is said to be the "life blood" of every business undertaking, be it large or medium or small scale enterprise. Inadequate finance was cited as a major problem by 34.35 per cent of women entrepreneurs.
- The procedures of bank loans, the delay and the running about involved discourages many a women from borrowing from banks. As the assistance from some government services and women groups is meagre, they are borrowing from the relatives and money lenders at high rate of interest. The rate of interest on money to be borrowed from money lenders was high according to 20.87 per cent of the women entrepreneurs.
- Another challenge facing the micro entrepreneurs is the nature of infrastructure, affecting 19.57 per cent of them. Poor infrastructure was a challenge cited by respondents, including Internet, web site, e-mail address, advertisement, etc.
- The inadequate availability of land, plots, and premises, irregular supply of enough inputs, inadequate technical support of production identification, and lack of upgradation of technology research and development and quality control, poor inventory management. The poor quality of management was cited as a major problem by 20.43 per cent of the women entrepreneurs.
- Women entrepreneurs have to face some particular problems like inadequate water supply, inadequate power supply, lack of communication facilities, etc. Remaining 10 per cent of the women entrepreneurs had stated that the inadequate power supply problems affect the women entrepreneurship in Pudukkottai district.

Suggestions for prospects of women entrepreneurs

Promoting entrepreneurship among women is especially important to tackle the problems of under-employment and unemployment in the society. The following measures are suggested to help women to seize various opportunities and face challenges in business.

- Education is a boon to mankind. As such, women should be considered as a specific target group for all development programmes. Government should extend better educational facilities and schemes to women folk. Adequate training programmes on management skills should be provided to women in every community.
- Educational institutes should tie up with various government and non-government agencies to assist in entrepreneurship development mainly to plan business projects.
- Vocational training is to be extended to women so as to enable them to understand the production process and production management.
- Training programmes may be organised to develop professional competencies in managerial, leadership, marketing, financial, production process, profit planning, maintaining books of accounts and other skills. This will encourage women to undertake business.
- International, national and local trade fairs, industrial exhibitions, seminars and conferences should be organised to facilitate interaction of aspiring women entresprneesurs with other women entrepreneurs.
- Women in business should be offered soft loans and subsides for encouraging them into industrial activities. Financial institutions should provide more working capital assistance both for micro and small scale women enterprises.
- Government should provide better infrastructure facilities and schemes for women folk. There should be continuous monitoring, improvement of training programmes, practical experience and personality development programmes to improve their overall personality standards.

- Finance is the main factor for any enterprise. The banking system is not sufficiently responsive to social banking needs and has not been able to deal with barriers that hinder women from using or gaining access to credit. Adequate arrangements must be made for the supply of credit facility at concessional rates for women entrepreneurs, in view of their growing needs.
- A Guidance Cell should be set up for woman entrepreneurs all over the state to handle their various problems.
- Positive attitudinal changes in the society recognising the role of women as entrepreneurs may lead to the situation in which women will be able to exploit their entrepreneurial talents.

Thus by adopting the foregoing suggestions in letter and spirit the problems associated with women entrepreneurship can be solved.

Conclusion

Women entrepreneurship has been recognised as an important source of economic growth. Women entrepreneurs create new jobs for themselves and others too. They also provide the society with different solutions to management, organisation and business problems. However, they still represent a minority of all entrepreneurs. Women entrepreneurs often face gender- based barriers in starting and growing their businesses, like lack of access to formal finance mechanisms; limited mobility and access to information networks and infrastructural facilities. Women entrepreneurship can make a strong contribution to the economic well-being of the family and community. However, highly educated, technically sound and professionally qualified women should be encouraged to manage their own business, rather than depend on wage employment outlets. The unexplored talents of young women can be identified, trained and used for various types of enterprises to increase the productivity in the industrial sector. Women entrepreneur networks are major sources of knowledge regarding entrepreneurship among women and they are increasingly recognised as a valuable tool for development and promotion of women entrepreneurs, particularly in poverty reduction and women empowerment, thus contributing to the Millennium Development Goals (MDGs).

4

Women Entrepreneurship and Employment in Micro and Small Manufacturing Enterprise

Narendra Jena

Abstract

Based on three rounds (51st, 56th & 62nd) of NSS surveys on unorganised manufacturing sector, the present paper attempts to analyse the changing trend, pattern of female entrepreneurship and employment in the unorganised manufacturing sector. Although there has been an increase in both female entrepreneurship and employment during the study period, i.e., 1994-95 to 2005-06, it has largely been concentrated in low-productive and labour intensive industry groups; female-owned enterprises are operating at low levels of productivity as compared to their male counterparts; further, a large part of female employment is part-time and contractual in nature and a preponderant majority of female are engaged in the tiniest enterprises, i.e., OAMEs. The present paper makes an attempt to understand the role of women in the unorganised manufacturing sector and calls for suitable policy interventions to improve their levels of earning and conditions of work.

Key Words: *Unorganised manufacturing, women, employment, entrepreneurship.*

Introduction

Decent employment has been an issue of serious concern in India, especially after the economic reforms. This concern is underlined not just by the fact that even the economy is growing at a fairly high rate, but that the employment situation has been nevertheless discouraging. The overall employment has been growing at a very slower pace and the conditions of employment have also been far from satisfactory. Another serious concern relating to employment has been the rise of employment opportunities only in the unorganised or informal segment of the economy, which is largely characterised by low levels of wages, insecure and poor quality of employment. In such a scenario, the issue of women employment and entrepreneurship unveils another dimension of the employment challenge which is not frequently discussed in the Indian context.

There is a general view in the literature that the rate of economic growth and level of education have a significant positive impact on female employment. But it is also argued that female participation in the labour market has been low due to various factors such as limited entitlement to resources and assets, social institutions, inadequate access to education and training, limited freedom to move and so on. Women are generally discouraged from acquiring relevant skills and human capital required to enter into the labour market (Papola 1999). Therefore, the presence of female in well-paid and regular jobs in the organised sector is very low (Mitra 2006).

In addition to limited employment opportunities for females, there are serious signs of gender discrimination in terms of wages, job security, conditions of work, occupational safety and so on. Another important issue in this discussion is the failure of government statistics to capture the picture of women's employment adequately and hence their leading to its non-recognition and under-estimation. There is an 'invisibility' of women's work in the official statistics due to their incapability to capture the figures. Women, though engaged in multiple economic activities, often fail to be a part of the market economy, since a large portion of their work remains unpaid (Sunder 1981).

However, the recent evidences show that there has been significant improvement in the incidence of female employment. While female employment has traditionally been concentrated in agriculture, recent studies have highlighted the overall increase in the presence of women in the labour market and their rising share both in rural and urban areas and in non-agricultural activities as well (Himansu 2011; Neetha 2009, 2010; Mehta 2010; Mitra 2006). In the secondary sector, for instance, the share of rural female employment has increased from 6.7 per cent in 1977-78 to 13.0 per cent in 2009-10, whereas the share of urban female employment has increase in the from 32.4 per cent to 33.4 per cent during the same period (Himanshu 2011). But since a large part of India's manufacturing is comprised of unorganised segment, an incisive and elaborate understanding of this category of workers is thus essential to comprehend India's labour market especially from the point of view of income generation and poverty reduction.

The present paper thus attempts a detailed account of female entrepreneurship and employment in the unorganised manufacturing sector in India. It analyses the pattern and magnitude of female employment; whether female-owned enterprises generate more female employment than their male counterpart; whether the female-owned enterprises are more productive than male-owned enterprises; what is the nature of female employment and so on. The data source for the study is National Sample Survey Organisation (NSSO) survey on unorganised manufacturing in its 51st (1994-95), 56th (2000-01) and 62nd (2005-06) rounds. A major problem that needs to be solved while comparing the NSS rounds is the choice of National Industrial Classification (NIC). The concordance table has been used to compare different NSS rounds and the nineteen 2-digit industries are re-classified into 15 industry groups across various rounds following the NIC 1987. The concordance table is given in the appendix.

Female employment situation: recent trends

Recent data shows that female employment has increased in the secondary sector and tertiary sector during 1993-94 to 2009-10. However, the increased female employment in secondary sector is evident from the rural and urban areas. In fact, rural female employment in secondary sector increased from 8.7 million in 1993-94 to 13.6 million in 2009-10 whereas urban female employment in this sector increased from 4.5 million to 7.2 million during the same period of time (refer to table-1).

Table - 1: Latest trends in work force (in millions)

Year	Rural male			Rural female		
	Primary	*Secondary*	*Tertiary*	*Primary*	*Secondary*	*Tertiary*
1993-94	139.1	21.0	27.6	90.3	8.7	5.8
2004-05	145.5	33.9	39.4	103.3	12.6	8.2
2009-10	145.9	44.8	41.3	83.1	13.6	8.0
	Urban male			Urban female		
1993-94	5.8	21.2	37.5	4.3	4.5	6.2
2004-05	5.5	31.1	53.8	4.5	7.3	9.8
2009-10	6.0	34.7	59.4	3.2	7.2	10.3

Source: Himanshu (2011), p. 46.

Table - 2: Distribution of workers by industrial groups (in %)

Year	Rural male			Rural female		
	Primary	*Secondary*	*Tertiary*	*Primary*	*Secondary*	*Tertiary*
1993-94	74.1	11.2	14.7	86.2	8.3	5.5
2004-05	66.5	15.5	18	83.3	10.2	6.6
2009-10	62.8	19.3	17.8	79.3	13	7.6
	Urban male			Urban female		
1993-94	9	32.9	58.1	24.7	29.1	46.2
2004-05	6.1	34.4	59.5	18.1	32.4	49.5
2009-10	6	34.6	59.3	13.9	33.3	52.8

Source: Himanshu (2011), p. 46.

The expansion of rural female employment in secondary sector had raised its share from 8.3 per cent in 1993-94 to 13.0 per cent in 2009-10, whereas urban female employment in this sector had increased its share from 29.1 per cent to 33.3 per cent during the same period (table-2).

The rise in female employment is often explained by improvement in female educational attainment. Sharmila and Christoper (2010) found that there had been significant progress in the performance of women's education attainment as is evident from the rising female literacy rates over time. Besides, the last decade had witnessed the rise of micro finance institutions and self-help groups (SHGs) which have not only opened greater employment and entrepreneurship opportunities for the female but also enhanced their empowerment. Ramesh (2007) observed that over 300 lakh women were linked to banks through over 22 lakh SHGs.

Increased presence of women in the labour market does show some signs of comfort, but does it reflect a demand-led expansion of productive employment opportunities or an outcome of the search for survival strategies? Sadly, a large part of the expansion in female employment is mostly subsistent in nature and distress-driven due to lack of gainful employment opportunities. Because agriculture, the largest employer has witnessed serious employment setbacks especially after the economic reforms. The rise in the share of female employment in manufacturing and services is therefore partly due to poor performance of agriculture. Further, during the recent year increase in sub-contracting and outsourcing activities in manufacturing has promoted the role of home-based work especially among women. But these activities again are of part-time and contractual and low productive nature. Nearly 36 per cent of the female own account proprietors were home-workers, operating on contract or sub-contract arrangements (NCEUS 2007). In addition, service sector provides a significant employment to women workers, but their concentration in personal services in urban areas points towards distress-driven employment growth (Mehta 2010).

Since a large part of women employment is contractual in home-work/home- based work and a significantly high proportion of unorganised manufacturing enterprises operate inside the household premises, it will be interesting to understand the dynamic changes, the pattern of female employment and entrepreneurship in the unorganised manufacturing sector in the context of changing economic situation. Followed by the introduction, section II analyses the overall female participation in the Indian economy; section III briefly discusses the size, structure and growth of the unorganised manufacturing sector; while section IV analyses the pattern of female entrepreneurship and productivity differences in female and male owned enterprises. Section V describes the trend, pattern and growth of female employment in the unorganised manufacturing sector. The concluding section, (Section VI) presents a summary of the paper and suggest some policy measures towards increasing the employment opportunities for female and improving their levels of earning and conditions of work.

Size, structure and growth of unorganised manufacturing sector

The manufacturing sector, contributing 15.6 per cent to GDP (organised = 10.4 and unorganised= 5.2 per cent), is growing at a rate of 8.9 per cent and had emerged as a fast growing segment of India's domestic economy in 2008-09 (NAS 2010). The unorganised manufacturing sector, contributing one-third of value added and nearly 80 per cent of manufacturing employment, also accounts for the bulk of manufacturing exports1.

The total number of enterprises in the unorganised manufacturing sector had increased from 93.4 lakhs million in 1994-95 to 121.2 lakhs in 2005-06 in the rural areas (table-3). During the same period, the total number of enterprises in the unorganised manufacturing sector in the urban areas had increased from 29.6 lakhs to 4.94 lakhs.

That is, enterprises of all sizes had grown at varying rate both in rural and urban areas. However, more than 90 per cent of the rural and nearly 70 per cent of the urban enterprises were comprised of OwnAccount Manufacturing Enterprises (OAMEs) which is the smallest among the three types of units in the unorganised manufacturing sector.

As far as employment in the unorganised manufacturing sector is concerned, the total number of workers engaged in rural areas had increased from 205.2 lakhs in 1994-95 to 234.5 lakhs in 2005-06 (table-3).

Table - 3: Number and distribution of enterprises and workers in unorganised manufacturing sector by enterprise type

Year		No. in lakh		% share					
				Rural			Urban		
		Rural	Urban	OAME	NDME	DME	OAME	NDME	DME
1994-95	Enterprises	93.4	29.6	90.56	6.31	3.14	66.69	22.14	11.17
	Workers	205.2	90.0	80.18	7.92	11.9	42.03	25.11	32.86
2000-01	Enterprises	119.3	5.08	92.65	5.28	2.07	70.88	21.26	7.86
	Workers	23.98	130.9	79.83	8.06	12.12	45.16	27.71	27.12
2005-06	Enterprises	121.2	49.4	91.6	6.14	2.26	70.9	20.74	8.36
	Workers	234.5	129.8	76.82	10.16	13.01	43.64	26.15	30.21

Source: Computed using NSS unit level data 51st, 56th and 62nd round on unorganised manufacturing.

During the same period, the employment in urban areas had also increased from 90 lakhs to 129 lakhs. It shows that a significant section of population in both rural and urban areas depends on the unorganised manufacturing sector for livelihood. The unorganised manufacturing has thus emerged as a major source of income and livelihood for rural population.

During 1994-95 to 2005-06 the share of workers employed in OAME units in rural areas had declined and that of NDME and DME had increased. In fact, the share of workers in OAME units had marginally declined from 80.18 per cent in 1994-95 to 76.82 per cent in 2005-06, while the share of workers in NDME units had increased from 7.92 per cent to 10.16 per cent during the same period. Further, the share of rural workers employed in DME units had increased from 11.90 per cent in 1994-95 to 13.01 per cent in 2005-06. This may be due to modernisation of small scale industries.

Female entrepreneurship pattern in unorganised manufacturing sector

Entrepreneurship contributes in various ways to economic development and job creation. Entrepreneurship emerges from an individual's creative spirit into long term business ownership, job creation, and economic security. Women entrepreneurs may be defined as the women or a group of women who initiate, organise and operate a business enterprise.

The hidden entrepreneurial potentials of women have gradually been changing with the growing sensitivity to the role and economic status of women in the society. During the last decade, women entrepreneurship has come to be seen as an important untapped source of economic growth. Women entrepreneurs create new jobs for themselves and others. And, being different from their male counterparts, they also provide the society with different solutions to management, organisation and business problems as well as to the exploitation of entrepreneurial opportunities. Even so, the topic of women in entrepreneurship has been largely neglected.

There are many constraints for Indian women entrepreneurs. These are socio-cultural barriers, lack of confidence, market oriented risk, motivational factors and awareness about the available financial assistance. Major problems faced by women entrepreneurs during the reference period, were poor location of the unit, tough competition from larger and established units, lack of transport facility, lack of time for household work, non- availability of raw material, etc.

Changes in policies have a significant differential impact on women workers within such a socio-economic framework. The liberalisation policies have changed the nature of female entrepreneurship in the unorganised manufacturing sector.

Internationally, feminisation has resulted in a perceptible rise in female labour force participation in the face of a fall in male participation (Deshpande & Deshpande 1992). Since tightening of production cost is very important, labour market regulations are viewed as 'rigidities' since they raise the costs and thereby have a harmful effect on the growth of future employment. This changed perception of protective labour legislation and social security measures was ushered in in the era of deregulation. These changes have an impact on the ownership pattern of enterprises in the unorganised manufacturing sector.

An OAME is an undertaking run by the household members, usually without any hired worker. In other words, in the case of

OAMEs, owners are themselves the workers, operating with the help of family members. Since majority of the enterprises studied were OAMEs, it is appropriate to look over the ownership pattern of the enterprises. There has been a significant change in the nature and sectoral distribution of ownership pattern of enterprises in the unorganised manufacturing sector. Table-4 shows the proportion of enterprises owned by females.

Table - 4: Percentage of enterprises owned by females

	1994 - 95	*2000 - 01*	*2005 - 06*
Rural	15.74	25.9 8	37.65
Urban	12.07	26.40	34.64
Total	14.72	26.11	36.78

Source: Computed using NSS unit level data 56th and 62nd round on unorganised manufacturing.

The percentage of enterprises owned by females had increased from 14.72 per cent in 1994-95 per cent to 36.78 per cent in 2005-06 (table 4). This is true of enterprises located in both rural and urban areas. It can be observed that there is thus a feminisation of ownership pattern among enterprises in the unorganised manufacturing sector. The increasing trend of female owned enterprises may, however, be explained by both pull and push factors. First, the percentage of enterprises owned by females in rural areas had increased from 15.74 per cent in 1994-95 to 37.65 per cent in 2005-06 (table-4). During the same period, the percentage of enterprises owned by females in urban areas too had increased from 12.07 per cent to 34.78 per cent. Further, the 2-digit level analysis also supports this argument.

Table - 5: Industry-wise distribution of female owned unorganised manufacturing enterprises by location

NIC	Rural		Urban		Total	
	2000-01	**2005-06**	**2000-01**	**2005-06**	**2000-01**	**2005-06**
20-21	6.02	5.18	6.68	5.01	6.22	5.14
22	35.30	38.22	24.25	21.07	31.96	33.55
23+ 24+ 25	7.67	6.0 6	7.89	6.30	7.73	6.12
26	28 .87	31.97	37.49	47.52	31.48	36.21

(Contd...)

27	14.51	9.02	2.56	2.04	10.90	7.12
28	0.34	2.10	2.67	2.34	1.04	2.16
29	0.12	0.05	0.38	0.79	0.20	0.25
30	2.67	5.13	6.15	5.74	3.73	5.30
31	0.43	0.16	0.80	0.42	0.54	0.23
32	0.60	0.52	1.32	0.68	0.82	0.57
33	0.00	0.01	0.05	0.07	0.01	0.02
34	0.07	0.06	0.66	0.50	0.25	0.18
35 -3 6	0.04	0.03	0.43	0.44	0.16	0.14
37	0.00	0.00	0.04	0.47	0.01	0.13
38	3.34	1.49	8.63	6.61	4.94	2.89
ALL	100	100	100	100	100	100

Source: Computed using NSS unit level data 56th and 62nd round on unorganized manufacturing.

Tables-5 and 6 show the percentage share of female owned enterprises by 2-digit level industry divisions. Agro based industries were dominated by female ownership enterprises and their share had increased over time in both rural and urban areas. These industries included manufacture of textile products (26), manufacture of tobacco and beverage products (22) and manufacture of paper and paper products (28). There was a drastic change in the ownership pattern in paper and paper products units in rural areas during 2000-06. In fact, the percentage of enterprises owned by females had increased from 0.34 per cent in 2000-01 to 2.10 per cent in 2005-06. On the other hand, the share of enterprises owned by females in several non-agro industries had declined.

Table - 6: Industry-wise Distribution of Female Owned Unorganised Manufacturing Enterprises by Type of Enterprises

NIC	*OAME*		*NDME*		*DME*	
	2000-01	***2005-06***	***2000-01***	***2005-06***	***2000-01***	***2005-06***
20-21	5.83	4.87	24.21	18.42	11.54	10.55
22	32.72	34.26	2.18	4.41	2.73	0.75
23+24+25	7.59	5.90	12.64	16.09	16.41	14.98
26	31.50	36.35	33.21	37.83	21.62	11.78
27	11.09	7.20	3.99	3.41	1.93	3.74
28	0.94	2.09	4.97	5.64	6.39	4.40

(Contd...)

29	0.19	0.22	0.53	0.19	1.11	4.62
30	3.77	5.38	0.71	0.67	6.37	4.86
31	0.50	0.18	2.30	1.37	2.25	4.56
32	0.74	0.51	3.20	2.46	7.40	4.35
33	0.00	0.01	0.39	0.08	0.83	0.98
34	0.12	0.06	3.71	3.57	12.10	8.95
35-36	0.08	0.08	2.92	2.32	4.55	4.31
37	0.00	0.02	0.23	0.09	0.72	17.66
38	4.95	2.87	4.79	3.46	4.04	3.50
ALL	100	100	100	100	100	100

Source: Computed using NSS unit level data 56th and 62nd round on unorganized manufacturing.

These industries included manufacture of rubber, petroleum and petroleum products (31), non-metallic mineral products (32), basic metal alloys (33), machinery and equipments (35-36), and transport equipments (37). However, as seen from table-6, female owned DME enterprises in transport equipments industry had increased during 2000-06. The highest percentage share of female owned OAME and NDME units was in the textile products industry group (26) among all industries, whereas the highest percentage share of female owned DME units was in transport equipments industry group (37).

Table - 7: Ratio of GVA per workers in female-owned enterprises to male-owned enterprises (in %)

NIC	*2000-01*				*2005-06*			
	OAME	*NDME*	*DME*	*All*	*OAME*	*NDME*	*DME*	*All*
20-21	0.62	0.83	1.35	0.63	0.46	0.80	1.14	0.46
22	0.67	0.76	0.88	0.65	0.89	0.33	1.13	0.82
23+24+25	0.64	0.97	1.39	0.54	0.44	0.57	1.19	0.38
26	0.39	1.02	1.13	0.38	0.41	0.76	1.10	0.38
27	0.31	0.81	0.92	0.29	0.26	1.14	1.37	0.24
28	0.22	0.64	0.94	0.25	0.42	0.88	0.83	0.34
29	0.37	1.04	0.99	0.42	0.39	0.86	0.93	0.44

(Contd...)

30	0.33	0.74	0.54	0.24	0.66	0.22	0.68	0.31
31	0.24	1.16	0.99	0.29	0.35	1.85	0.99	0.57
32	0.69	0.58	1.34	0.72	0.82	0.58	1.02	0.73
33	0.66	0.95	1.31	1.30	0.14	0.96	0.51	0.42
34	0.77	1.14	1.07	1.27	1.20	0.96	1.08	1.54
35-36	0.43	0.86	0.78	0.79	0.59	0.97	0.91	0.90
37	0.62	1.12	0.76	0.91	0.48	1.56	0.88	1.08
38	0.26	0.85	0.72	0.26	0.24	0.36	1.48	0.20
All	0.43	0.86	1.10	0.39	0.42	0.67	1.12	0.35

Source: Computed using NSS unit level data 56th and 62nd round on unorganised manufacturing.

Table-7 presents the ratio of GVA per worker in female owned enterprises to male owned enterprises. It shows that the overall GVA per worker in female owned enterprises is one-third (0.35 %) of male owned enterprises in all, but is 12 per cent higher in DME units. Further, it had declined for OAME and NDME units and marginally increased for DME units during 2000-01 to 2005-06. In addition, the ratio of GVA per worker in female owned enterprises to male owned enterprises in DME units has increased from 6 industry groups to 8 during the same period of time. This may be due to the access to capital and resources which encourages women entrepreneurs to perform better. As far as OAME and NDME units are concerned lack of capital, lack of other facilities were the constraints to women entrepreneurs' doing better.

It is observed that the GVA per worker in female owned enterprises to male owned enterprises has declined in food and food product industries (20-21), textile industry (23+24+25), wood and wood products industries (27) during 2000-01 to 2005-06. Particularly, the decline was more in OAME units. From this, it is clear that the increase in female entrepreneurship does not lead to increase in labour productivity in these enterprises. Although the GVA per worker in female owned enterprises was better in metal industries, there was low female employment in this industry group.

It was also observed that there were significant rural-urban contrasts in the pattern of labour productivity in female- vis-à-vis male-owned enterprises. But does the increase in female entrepreneurship also lead to feminisation of employment in unorganised manufacturing sector? This is discussed in the next section.

Female employment in unorganised manufacturing sector

Women engaged in unorganised manufacturing activity in India constitute a large and significant section of our population. In fact, women workers in the unorganised sector are predominantly (about 48%) concentrated in manufacturing (NCEUS 2007). However, there had been persistent expansion of the unorganised sector in India since the implementation of the new economic policy. The reasons may be the rate and pattern of growth, including the labour intensity and sectoral composition of growth, economic restructuring or economic crisis, including privatisation of public enterprises and cut-backs in public expenditures, and global integration of the economy, including the restructuring of global production characterised by outsourcing or sub-contracting. In today's globalising world, various demand factors are also at work. An increasing share of unorganised work is sub-contracted from the formal sector. The low costs of sub-contracted work contribute to profits in the formal sector. In their pursuit of global competitiveness, employers in a wide range of key export industries favour the kinds of employment relations associated, rightly or wrongly, with women, namely those with insecure contracts, low wages, and few benefits. Self-employed women producers are also affected by current trends. Given the rapid shifts in market demand, both domestically and globally, self-employed women producers find it difficult to retain their traditional market niche or negotiate access to emerging markets. There is also evidence to suggest that global integration and competition are associated with the erosion of both the employment arrangements of workers and the competitiveness of micro businesses.

There is evidence of feminisation of workers in unorganised manufacturing sector both in rural and urban areas. In fact, the rural female workers employed in unorganised manufacturing sector had increased from 37.85 per cent in 1994-95 to 43.92 per cent in

2005-06. During the same period the urban female workers had increased from 17.46 per cent to 27.26 per cent (refer to table-8).

Table - 8: Share of female workers in the unorganised manufacturing sector, 1994/5-2005/6 (in %)

	Rural	*Urban*	*Total*
1994-95	37.85	17.46	31.05
2000-01	38.69	24.58	33.71
2005-06	43.92	27.26	37.98

Source: Computed using NSS unit level data 51st, 56th and 62nd round on unorganised manufacturing.

There is a sharp decline of male employment during 2000-01/2005-06 in both rural and urban areas (table-9). The decline of male employment during the same period in rural and urban areas may be due to low remuneration which discourages the male workers to engage in this sector. The other reason may be the availability of employment opportunities in other sectors.

There has been a faster growth in the employment of females than males during the years 2000 to 2005, in both rural and urban areas, thus raising the proportion of women workers in this sector. In fact, female workers employed in unorganised manufacturing sector were growing at 7.23 per cent in rural areas and at 24.02 per cent in urban areas during 2000-05 (table-9). The growth in numbers of female workers in both rural and urban areas is both for full time and part-time work. Employment prospects for women are also found to be associated with flexibility. Flexibility of enterprises implies sub-contracting form of production.

Table 9: Share of female workers in the unorganised manufacturing sector, 1994/5-2005/6 (in %)

	Rural			*Urban*			*Total*		
	Male	*Female*	*Persons*	*Male*	*Female*	*Persons*	*Male*	*Female*	*Persons*
1994-2000	1.12	1.73	1.35	1.29	8.86	2.83	1.19	3.26	1.86
2000-05	-6.87	7.23	-0.44	-18.55	24.02	-0.17	-10.85	12.58	-0.35

Source: Computed using NSS unit level data 51st, 56th and 62nd round on unorganised manufacturing.

The feminisation of employment in unorganised manufacturing sector was in the form of increase in the share of female workers compared to male workers. Table-10 shows the percentage share of female employment in rural and urban areas by industry divisions, of the National Industrial Classification (NIC) 1987 workers into two successive periods: 2000-01 and 2005-06.

Agro based industries are dominated by providing female employment and its share has increased over time in rural and urban areas. These industries include the manufacture of tobacco and beverages (22), manufacture of textile products (23+24+25), manufacture of paper and paper products (28). On the other hand, female employment in non-agro industries had declined in rural and urban areas which include the manufacture of non- metallic mineral products (32), basic metal alloys (33), machinery and equipments (35-36), and transport equipments (37). Non- agro industries are capital intensive and require regular skill formation. Further, female workers were unable to manage the burden of work in non-agro industries. Second, some employers reduced male employment and increased female employment. In addition, feminisation of workers in the unorganised manufacturing sector is supported by the analysis of type of the work.

Table - 10: Share of female workers across industries in rural and urban areas (in %)

NIC	*Rural*		*Urban*		*Total*	
	2000-01	*2005-06*	*2000-01*	*2005-06*	*2000-01*	*2005-06*
20-21	28.04	28.85	21.47	23.70	26.43	27.68
22	64.31	72.14	71.20	71.27	65.68	71.98
23+24+25	49.30	52.46	33.17	30.27	42.71	40.87
26	41.64	51.84	28.34	38.05	35.88	46.33
27	34.47	34.69	10.95	11.57	30.20	30.36
28	34.54	67.26	16.35	22.66	19.29	36.65
29	9.49	11.03	11.67	13.00	10.94	12.62
30	45.64	72.40	60.64	63.74	52.61	69.75

(Contd...)

31	28.87	31.85	17.11	18.36	20.65	23.07
32	34.71	29.42	31.68	24.02	34.22	28.56
33	8.23	7.87	2.82	6.81	4.60	7.12
34	12.89	8.40	4.08	3.86	7.84	5.81
35-36	10.58	8.49	8.70	5.49	9.20	6.25
37	5.46	3.52	2.26	3.84	2.71	3.74
38	35.84	27.22	18.26	16.65	24.62	19.97
ALL	38.69	43.92	24.59	27.26	33.71	37.98

Source: Computed using NSS unit level data 51st, 56th and 62nd round on unorganised manufacturing.

Looking at the distribution of overall employment by nature of work, the share of female in both full time and part-time work had increased. Table-12 shows that the percentage of female full time workers had increased from 23.91 per cent in 2000-01, though by a small extent, to 26.42 per cent in 2005-06. During the same period the percentage of female part-time workers had increased from 9.80 per cent to 11.56 per cent. The same trend is observed both in rural and urban areas. However, the incidence of part-time employment among the females was higher as compared to their male counterparts.

Table - 11: Share of female workers across industries by type of enterprises (in %)

NIC	*OAME*		*NDME*		*DME*	
	2000-01	*2005-06*	*2000-01*	*2005-06*	*2000-01*	*2005-06*
20-21	12.94	9.01	24.50	16.69	13.55	32.60
22	22.45	28.39	2.08	4.33	9.82	1.63
23+24+25	11.28	7.91	19.04	29.89	14.63	15.21
26	21.48	28.34	25.57	26.04	12.84	13.35
27	16.29	12.28	4.28	2.15	1.77	1.74
28	0.90	1.88	3.54	4.06	2.18	2.44
29	0.28	0.32	0.77	0.39	0.93	1.65
30	2.25	4.27	1.40	1.33	3.99	6.54
31	0.33	0.22	1.57	2.37	2.42	2.20
32	6.08	3.77	6.84	4.69	28.80	14.69

(*Contd*...)

33	0.05	0.03	0.25	0.30	0.07	0.25
34	0.92	0.57	2.32	1.86	1.06	1.28
35-36	0.20	0.17	1.47	2.50	3.57	1.60
37	0.01	0.02	0.22	0.15	0.17	0.37
38	4.54	2.82	6.15	3.26	4.21	4.44
ALL	100	100	100	100	100	100

Source: Computed using NSS unit level data 56th and 62nd round on unorganised manufacturing.

Table - 12: Share of female workers an0y nature of employment (in %)

	2000-01					2005-06				
	Female		Male			Female		Male		
	Full time	*Part time*	*Full time*	*Part time*	*ALL*	*Full time*	*Part time*	*Full time*	*Part time*	*ALL*
Rural	27.01	11.68	53.91	7.4	100	30.55	13.37	48.08	8	100
Urban	18.22	6.37	72.23	3.19	100	18.97	8.29	68.89	3.85	100
Total	23.91	9.8	60.38	5.91	100	26.42	11.56	55.5	6.52	100

Source: Computed using NSS unit level data 51st 56th and 62nd round on unorganised manufacturing.

Table - 13: Distribution of female workers by nature of employment in unorganised manufacturing sector (in %)

	2000-01				2005-06			
	Fulltime		Parttime		Fulltime		Parttime	
	Female	*Male*	*Female*	*Male*	*Female*	*Male*	*Female*	*Male*
Rural	33.38	66.62	61.21	38.79	38.85	61.15	62.56	37.44
Urban	20.14	79.86	66.64	33.36	21.59	78.41	68.28	31.72
Total	28.36	71.64	62.38	37.62	32.26	67.74	63.93	36.07

Source: Computed using NSS unit level data 51st 56th and 62nd round on unorganised manufacturing.

The male-female division of full and part time employment also suggests that there has been a faster increase in full time than part time employment of workers as is shown by a large variations in their share in the former than latter. While the share of female in full time employment increased from 28.36 per cent to 32.26 per cent and that of part time employment increased from 62.38 per cent to 63.93 per cent during 2000/2006. This holds true both for rural and urban areas (refer to table 13).

Does increase in female employment relate to increase in sub-contracting? Sub- contracting represents a form of inter-firm relationship where large firms procure manufactured components, sub-assemblies and products from a large number of small firms. In some cases, sub-contracting is associated with 'job work' where a parent firm provides the necessary raw materials to small firms which return these materials after turning them into a required form (as per the technical specification), at a pre-determined rate. The percentage of unorganised manufacturing enterprises operating on contract basis had increased from 30.66 per cent in 2000-01 to 31.68 per cent in 2005-06 (table-14).

Table - 14: Percentage of enterprises working on contract basis (in %)

	2000-01				*2005-06*			
	OAME	*NDME*	*DME*	*Total*	*OAME*	*NDME*	*DME*	*Total*
% of enterprises working under sub-contracting								
All	26.43	2.91	1.32	30.66	27.82	2.63	1.22	31.68
Distribution of subcontract in enterprises(%)								
Rural	94.25	4.11	1.64	100	94.06	4.47	1.47	100
Urban	72.51	18.65	8.84	100	74.44	16.55	9.00	100
All	86.21	9.49	4.30	100	87.84	8.30	3.86	100

Source: Computed using NSS unit level data 56th and 62nd round on unorganised manufacturing.

It is evident that the incidence of sub-contracting was more among the smaller sized enterprises, i.e., OAME and those located in rural areas (table-14). The fact that there is a possibility of penetration by merchant capital in search of cheap home-based production sources that ensure the required returns. Most of the units were getting inputs from the parent enterprise and there was little choice for the household units to bargain.

One of the common exploitative practices adopted by the middlemen is to deduct wages for 'rejection'. Many a time, the middlemen withhold part of the payment to maintain a hold on the worker and to discourage him/her from leaving for competitors. The strategy of denying work to the most vocal leader amongst the workers is often adopted by the traders. The home workers tend to remain with the same contractor, even in the absence of written agreements or benefit payments. The inertia in seeking alternatives is accounted for by the high opportunity costs of change (lack of alternative or excess supply of labour), debt bondage, delayed payments, and contractors preferring to keep workers isolated (Mehrotra and Biggeri 2007). The majority of these home workers are women.

Table - 15: Percentage of female workers working in sub-contracting enterprise (in %)

NIC	OAME		NDME		DME		ALL	
	2000-01	2005-06	2000-01	2005-06	2000-01	2005-06	2000-01	2005-06
20-21	4.57	7.80	11.73	3.87	7.51	0.87	5.40	5.74
22	84.68	66.93	10.18	46.28	10.37	26.11	80.83	66.53
23+24+25	55.82	52.64	66.05	65.38	52.85	46.81	56.12	53.52
26	31.83	40.87	44.55	26.99	51.27	45.84	33.66	40.52
27	5.65	3.92	10.29	6.40	7.37	55.76	5.73	4.71
28	41.46	73.62	48.86	28.40	40.69	57.77	42.26	67.91
29	42.18	64.89	27.95	34.69	65.10	53.51	46.72	59.89
30	79.73	80.58	8.03	0.15	28.11	11.64	69.51	69.93
31	50.38	38.58	29.13	45.13	35.29	18.81	41.93	31.89
32	4.43	10.01	13.67	6.14	3.73	1.87	4.50	7.56
33	50.79	21.01	60.49	54.37	42.16	34.47	51.38	33.22
34	10.67	13.72	39.00	31.09	35.18	48.41	15.94	21.66
35-36	44.51	39.77	36.64	75.96	35.96	27.74	38.51	45.14
37	9.12	66.23	29.74	16.52	64.51	72.92	39.74	64.56
38	40.96	50.54	39.73	42.09	48.84	26.35	41.61	46.82
ALL	38.45	43.02	35.05	36.04	24.88	21.26	36.97	40.70

Source: Computed using NSS unit level data 56th and 62nd round on unorganised manufacturing.

Table-15 presents the percentage of female workers engaged in the sub-contracting units by the industry groups for each category of enterprises. The figures indicate that the importance of female employment in sub-contracting units had varied across industry groups.

Agro-based industries had dominated in terms of female employment in Indian unorganised manufacturing industry which operates under contract basis. Dominance of agro-based industries in terms of providing female employment (with more than 30 % share) belongs to manufacture of food and food products, beverages and tobacco products textiles and textile products industries. It is thus evident that industries extensively using sub-contracting include the ones that have female labour intensive production processes such as textiles and tobacco products. Correlation between total worker engaged in the unorganised manufacturing sector and female workers in sub-contracting enterprises has increased from 0.91 to 0.94.

Further, women workers in the unorganised manufacturing sector suffer under highly insecure and vulnerable working conditions. There are no social security measures to provide risk coverage and ensure the maintenance of basic living standards in times of crises such as unemployment or health issues. There are no laws to ensure they worked under suitable working conditions and are not subject to any health hazards. There is no fixity of working hours, no compliance to minimum wages and in most cases these are governed by local factors (NCEUS 2007). The insecurity, lack of safety, occupational hazards and incidence of exploitation is even more in the case of migrant labour and forced labour. This is because of lack of organisation and unionisation among the groups, which is mainly on account of the poor literacy and awareness levels and high levels of poverty prevalent among the groups. There is also very little legal protection available.

Conclusion

The present paper has attempted to examine the changing structure of female entrepreneurship and employment in the unorganised manufacturing sector. The analysis shows that there had been expansion in both female entrepreneurship and employment, but they were limited to a few agro-based industries. Increased presence of females in employment was also obtaining only in agro-based industries and among those operating under sub-contracting system. However, female-owned enterprises were operating at a low level of productivity as compared to male-owned enterprises. Further, females were engaged more in the tiniest enterprises, i.e., OAMEs and a large part of their employment opportunities were of part-time and contractual nature. Thus it reflects the precarious conditions of women in the unorganised manufacturing sector. The optimism about the current pattern of female entrepreneurship and employment is a cause for concern rather than cheer.

The analysis also shows that the changing policy environment has augmented the feminisation of employment in the unorganised manufacturing sector. Further, there is evidence of increase female entrepreneurship in this sector. In addition, the increase in female entrepreneurship did not lead to increase in labour productivity in these enterprises. This may be due to increase in the sub-contracting method of production. The GVA per worker in the female owned enterprises is one-third (0.35%) of male-owned enterprises in all, but is 12 per cent higher in DME units. Agro-based industries have dominated in terms of female employment in the Indian unorganised manufacturing industry which operates under contract basis.

In this context, policy intervention to increase labour productivity in unorganised manufacturing sector. It can be enhanced through public investment in physical capital as well as in human capital. The government should encourage and provide financial support to groups of small scale units for the purchase of machinery as also common facilities which individually they find unaffordable. Most workers continue to learn from the job, through informal training at their place of work, from low-skilled craft people. There is need for enhancing the skills and education of workers by reorienting the vocational education and training system. Micro enterprises need to be supported by better access to institutional finance through rural banking. In addition, marketing of products too needs to be supported.

Appendix

Concordance between 2-digit level of NIC-87 & appropriate level of NIC-98 (for converting NIC-98 based data in terms of NIC-87)

NIC 1987	Industry description	NIC 1987	NIC 1998
20-21	Food & food product industry	20-21	151 + 152 + 153 + 154
22	Beverage & tobacco industry	22	155 + 16
23 + 24 + 25	Textile industry	23 + 24 + 25	171
26	Textile product industry	26	172 + 173 + 181
27	Wood & wood product industry	27	20 + 361
28	Paper & paper product industry	28	21 + 22
29	Leather & leather product industry	29	182 + 19
30	Chemical & chemical product industry	30	24
31	Rubber, petroleum & petroleum-product industry	31	23 + 25
32	Non metallic mineral product industry	32	26
33	Basic metal alloys	33	27 + 371
34	Metal product	34	2811 + 2812 + 289
35-36	Machinery & equipments	35-36	2813 + 29 + 30 + 31 + 32
37	Transport equipments	37	34 + 35
38	Others	38	33 + 369
39		39	725

Source: National industrial classification, 1998, CSO.

5

Women in Small Businesses: A Study of Entrepreneurial Motivation

Anil Kumar
Parul

Abstract

As the economic development of any nation is found to be depending on businesses by women entrepreneurs as well among other factors, there is continuous need for the study of motivating factors with changing society patterns and increasing globalisation. Women from all age groups are found to be taking up the entrepreneurial activities and for each age group motivating factors are different. This paper throws light on the relationship between the motivating factors and age groups, with the help of tables. The data was collected from one hundred respondents through exploratory survey using a questionnaire. Statistical tools of mean and standard deviation were applied to the data to interpret the results. The paper is concluded by outlining the reasons for exploring motivations, implications, results and limitations, and setting a pathway for further research on the matter.

Key words: *Women entrepreneurship, age, motivation.*

Introduction

The economic development of any nation depends on the development of small businesses as much as on large business organisations. Among small businesses, those owned by women entrepreneurs contribute not only to economic development of the nation, but also strengthen the women segment of the society.

Women in India have always been engaged in home-based businesses like milk vending, ghee making, bangles making, cattle rearing, selling agricultural products, and shawl and fabric making. So women entrepreneurship in India is as old as the presence of such activities in this land. But modernisation of the society has enabled women to work outside the boundaries of home and get recognition as successful entrepreneurs. Indian women today are engaged in a vast variety of businesses. In cities, businesses by women are even found to be based on latest technologies. On a close look one can even notice that the variations are not just among the nature of business activities, but are seen in the age of women entrepreneurs. At each age interval a number of motivating factors are found to be affecting the nature of women entrepreneurs and for each age group different motivating factors are found to be the driving force. This paper is an attempt to closely diagnose the relation between these motivating factors among different age groups.

The paper is presented in five sections. Section one of the paper provides general introduction to entrepreneurship and motivation, while in the second section a brief review of the earlier literature is given. The third section states the objectives of the study, followed by research methodology. The fourth section presents the data analysis and interpretation thereof. The fifth and last section includes conclusions and limitations, and suggestions for future possibilities of research.

Entrepreneurship

Entrepreneurship is the purposeful activity of an individual or a group of associated individuals undertaken to initiate, maintain and aggrandise profit by production or distribution of economic goods and services. Thus entrepreneurship involves the functions of foreseeing investment and production opportunities, organising an enterprise to undertake a new production process, raising capital, hiring labour, arranging the supply of raw materials, finding site, introducing a new technique, discovering new resources or raw materials and selecting top managers for the daily operations of the enterprise. In this way it is obvious that entrepreneurship involves risk bearing, innovation, finding resources and opportunities, and making arrangements for operating an enterprise emerge as an important aspect and this task is achieved by an individual or a group of individuals. Thus, entrepreneurship refers to all the functions required to be performed in establishing an enterprise and the individual carrying out these functions is called the entrepreneur. In short, entrepreneur precedes entrepreneurship.

Motivation

Motivation refers to the way in which urges, drives, desires, striving, and aspirations or needs direct or control or explain the behaviour of a human being. The primary requisite of an entrepreneur is to give the best possible performance for the achievement of organisational goals. This performance is a function of ability and willingness of the entrepreneur. Ability depends on factors like education, experience and skill. But willingness to perform depends upon the level of motivation. Level of motivation in turn depends on the strength of needs, desires and aspirations of the entrepreneur. All these driving factors together constitute the motives. "Motive" gives direction to human behaviour to achieve the goals or fulfill the needs. Motive arouses and energises a person's activities. So motivation is something that moves a person to action and continues him in the course of action already initiated. Human behaviour is governed by needs and desires. Entrepreneurs feel motivated when their needs and expectation are satisfied as a result of working for the enterprise.

Review of literature

Jean Lee (1996) empirically analysed the responses from 110 out of 343 respondents using Manifest Needs Questionnaire (MNQ). He studied four need based motivation factors: achievement, affliction, autonomy and dominance among others. He also compared the characteristics of women entrepreneurs and women employees. Women entrepreneurs were found to be more aged, married, had children, signifying better work-life balance in comparison to women employees. The women entrepreneurs showed the highest need for achievement followed by affiliation, autonomy and dominance, and all these needs were of higher levels than in women employees. Level of education had the greatest effect on the need intensity among many factors affecting motivational needs.

Mishra & Bal (1997) conducted an empirical study on entrepreneurial motivation in seven districts of Orissa. The author had analysed the data collected from a sample of 110 entrepreneurs. Alarge number of factors - financial, institutional, cultural and political structure, overall socio-economic background, government policies, individuals' preferences and willingness - were found responsible for entrepreneurial activities in any country at any time. The behaviour of human beings is controlled by their urges, drives, desires and needs which are backed by motivational forces. The study revealed that desire for independence was the strongest motivational factor for entering into entrepreneurial business. Dissatisfaction with previous job, dependency situation, insistence by elders were strong compelling factors. Among the internal and external factors, business experience and liberal financial help from financial institutions emerged as major factors. Availability of raw materials, marketing support from government, accessibility of infrastructure and technology, moral support were some of the other major motivating factors.

Kaur and Bawa (1999) studied 100 middle class women entrepreneurs from Jalandhar, Ludhiana and Kapurthala cities in the state of Punjab. Value expectancy scale, Locus control Scale and Work Involvement Scale were used to gain insight into value orientation and motivational factors of women entrepreneurs. Ability utilisation scored the highest motivating factor followed by congenial work-conditions, achievement, advancement and aesthetic sense. In some cases death or ill health of the spouse was also a reason for starting business. Success rates among women with risk taking attitude and those having benefit of locus of control showed no significant differences. Personal characteristics were also quite similar. Besides, the study revealed that giving training to young ambitious women may further enhance their entrepreneurial skills as they are more prone to risky decisions.

Das M. (1999) conducted an exploratory study using in-depth personal interview method on women entrepreneurs in South India.

Information about business start up reason, success factor, age effect, problems, work-family conflict was gathered. Results showed that majority started business to keep themselves busy, to pursue their hobby and financial stability. Push factors relating to family circumstances played major role in starting business. Hard work, perseverance, quality product and services turned out to be reasons for success. More than 50 per cent started business from their own funds, faced working capital problems. 66 per cent had no previous business experience, also a major problem among others. 74 per cent women entrepreneurs reported about happy spouses and family pointing out lower level of work-family conflict.

Kalyani & Chandralekha (2000) studied the effect of various socio-economic and demographic characteristics on enterprise management of women entrepreneurs. The study was conducted in four districts of Andhra Pradesh. A sample of 300 women entrepreneurs was taken. The study revealed that the respondents who received support from husband and family were able to manage business activities effectively. Women entrepreneurs hailing from poor economic groups did not have much exposure to training. Majority of women did not have any business experience and were motivated by family members. Women seemed satisfied with their work and believed that business brought positivity in their life. Like educated women, illiterate women also practised different techniques for efficient management, but the educated women emphasised the importance of training. The author had suggested the need for multi-disciplinary developmental approach, and also recommended helping women entrepreneurs by developing ancillary units and linking them with bigger industrial units.

Sarri & Trihopoulou (2005) had examined personal characteristics and motivation of women entrepreneurs in Greece. The study revealed that the education level of the respondents was high; mostly women were married and had children. There was also a tendency to enter into business in old age. The women in Greece were mostly motivated by pull factors like self-fulfillment, need for creativity and independence.

Orhan and Scott (2001) surveyed 25 women entrepreneurs to explore the reasons that motivate women to enter into business. They used the qualitative research technique: the in-depth interview method to develop a model. Research indicated many motivating factors classified as influence of environment, push factors and pull factors. 'Dynastic compliance' and 'natural succession' were environmental influences. Push factors were 'no other choice' and 'forced entrepreneurs' Pull factors included 'informed entrepreneurs' and 'pure entrepreneurs'

Objectives and research methodology

The present study is an attempt towards finding the motivating factors responsible for the growth and development of women entrepreneurs at different age stages. The objective was to study the motivating factors affecting women entrepreneurs, to assess whether there was any difference in motivating factors affecting women of different age groups.

The data was collected for the study from 101 respondents. The survey was conducted in NCR region. (Gurgaon, Noida, Faridabad and New Delhi). The choice of cities was based on factors like development of the city, good system of rail and road networks, presence of private, good education system, public and cooperative banks, presence of training facilities, organisations, groups and networks that promote entrepreneurship. The women entrepreneurs that formed the sample were selected randomly keeping in mind the variation in age and businesses. The survey was done with the help of questionnaire based on Likert type five-degree scale from "extremely important" to "not at all". In total, eighteen statements were used to obtain the responses on motivational factors affecting women entrepreneurs of different age groups. Statistical tools like LSD, one way ANOVA, mean, standard deviation are used to analyse the collected data.

Hypotheses

The following hypotheses were framed and tested in respect of the factors influencing the women entrepreneurs.

H_{01} There is significant difference between women entrepreneurs of different age groups regarding their motive of need of money to engage in business.

H_{02} There is significant difference between women entrepreneurs of different age groups regarding their motive of job satisfaction to engage in business.

H_{03} There is significant difference between women entrepreneurs of different age groups regarding their motive of becoming a leader by engaging in business.

H_{04} There is significant difference between women entrepreneurs of different age groups regarding their motive of achieving high social status by engaging in business.

H_{05} There is significant difference between women entrepreneurs of different age groups regarding their motive of having own work-style and life-style by engaging in business.

H_{06} There is significant difference between women entrepreneurs of different age groups regarding their motive of earning respect by engaging in business.

H_{07} There is significant difference between women entrepreneurs of different age groups regarding their motive of utilisation of decision making skills by engaging in business.

H_{08} There is significant difference between women entrepreneurs of different age groups regarding their motive of providing security to family by engaging in business.

H_{09} There is significant difference between women entrepreneurs of different age groups regarding their motive of satisfaction of innovative instinct by engaging in business.

H_{010} There is significant difference between women entrepreneurs of different age groups regarding their motive of desire for more earnings by engaging in business.

H_{011} There is significant difference between women entrepreneurs of different age groups regarding their motive to be their own boss by engaging in business.

Data analysis

Each table shows age-wise distribution of women entrepreneurs and its association with each motivation variable among different age groups. For analysis, Age is divided into four classes: less than 30 years, 30-35 years, 35-40 years, and more than 40 years. Eighteen motivational factors were selected for this study.

Eleven of the respondents belonged to the age group 'less than 30', while 51 belonged to '30-35' years of age group, 25 fell under age the group '35-40', and 14 respondents were found to be of more than 40 years of age.

Table-1 shows the motive of women entrepreneurs to fulfill the need of money through business in different age groups. Need of money remains an important reason for women entrepreneurs to start a new business. However, among women of different age groups, the effect of motivation seemed to vary. The overall mean value (3.181) suggests that 'need for money' was considered a very important motivational factor by majority of women. Fewer women entrepreneurs were doing business for this reason in the age groups of 'less than 30' and 'more than 40' as compared to those in the age groups of 30-35 years and 35-40 years. It may be because mostly older women tend to work for recognition, leisure occupation, time pass, respect rather than money. For younger women the reasons may be to satisfy innovative instinct, to have additional pocket money, to gain recognition and so forth. F-value is statistically significant at 5 per cent level of significance.

Table - 1: Age and need of money

Age (in years)	*Need of money*				
	N	*Mean*	*SD*	*F-value*	*Significance level*
Less than 30	11	2 .3636	1 .0269	F test - 9 .842 df - 3	.000
30- 35	51	3 .2549	.8448		
35- 40	25	3 .0400	1 .0198		
More than 40	14	3 .8571	1 .0271		
Grand Total	101	3 .181	.9971		

Table - 2: Age and job satisfaction

Age (in years)	*Job satisfaction*				
	N	*Mean*	*SD*	*F-value*	*Significance level*
Less than 30	11	3.8182	.40452		
30- 35	51	3.5686	.67097	F test –	
35- 40	25	3.8000	.86603	7.859	.000
More than 40	14	4.4286	.51355	df - 3	
Grand Total	101	3.7723	.73323		

The distribution of women entrepreneurs of different age groups regarding achieving job satisfaction by engaging in business is presented in table-2. The overall mean value is 3.7723, which means that 'job satisfaction' plays an important part in motivating the women entrepreneurs. Job satisfaction was found to be extremely important for women entrepreneurs in higher age groups than in the lower age groups. It may be because older women preferred satisfaction and stability. For the age group of '35-40', the standard deviation of .86603 was maximum. It shows that perceptions of women entrepreneurs varied greatly on the Likert scale from 'extremely important' to 'not at all'. In the age group of 'less than 30' the standard deviation of .40452 was minimum, showing that majority of women had agreed that job satisfaction was very important motive for entrepreneurial activity. It also means that young women entrepreneurs were of less compromising nature and they worked hard for achieving satisfaction through their work. F-value at 7.859 is statistically significant at 5 per cent level of significance.

Table - 3: Age and motivational factor 'to become leader'

Age (in years)	*To be com e lea der*				
	N	*Mean*	*Std. deviation*	*F-value*	*Significance level*
Less than 30	11	3 .00	1.095 45		
30- 35	51	2.4 706	1.222 34	F test –	
35- 40	25	2.5 200	1.194 43	6 .787	.000
More than 40	14	3.2 857	1.540 66	df - 3	
Grand Total	101	2.6 535	1.268 35		

Table-3 shows variation of leadership motive among women entrepreneurs in different age groups. The overall mean value of 2.6535 suggests that for the respondents this variable was important. Desire for leadership was dominant among both the younger and the older women entrepreneurs as compared to middle age women entrepreneurs. Women in the age group of 'more than 40' enjoyed leadership. It gave them satisfaction about their work and satisfied their nurturing instincts. The mean value was the least in the age group of 30-35, implying that at middle age fewer women were inspired by this factor. This can be attributed to family responsibilities being maximum at this age. For the age group of 'less than 30', the mean value was 3, which shows that the respondents in this age group were more ambitious and they considered leadership as an important motivational factor. The least value of standard deviation in this age group points out that the level of agreement was higher in this age group as compared to other age groups. The F value of 6.787 is statistically significant at 5 per cent level of significance.

Table - 4: Age and motivational factor of 'High social status'

Age (in years)	*High social status*				
	N	*Mean*	*Std. deviation*	*F-value*	*Significance level*
Less than 30	11	3.818 2	.7 5076	F test - 5 .199 df - 3	
30- 35	51	3.196 1	1.2 8093		
35- 40	25	3.72	.7 3711		.003
More than 40	14	4.00	.9 6077		
Grand Total	101	3.505 0	1.1 1017		

The responses on the motive of women entrepreneurs in different age groups to achieve high social status through business are shown in table-4. The overall mean value was 3.50 suggesting that most of the respondents had considered social status as a very important motivational factor. Older women entrepreneurs seemed to enjoy high social status, and considered this factor as very important, so they tended to remain in business to maintain their status. The mean is also high (3.818) for the age group of 'less than 30' because women entrepreneurs in this age group were ambitious and wanted to achieve high status in society. The standard deviation in this age group also signified that women entrepreneurs in this age group had high level of agreement regarding 'social status' as an important motivational factor. For the age group of 30-35 years the mean value (3.196) was the lowest among all age groups and the SD (1.2809) was the highest. This shows that women entrepreneurs in this age group considered social status important but not as important as those in other age groups. Their views showed high variation on the importance scale. The F value of 5.199 is statistically significant at 5 per cent level of significance.

Table - 5: Age and motivational factor 'Own work-style and life-style'

Age (in years)	*Own work-style and life-style*				
	N	*Mean*	*Std. deviation*	*F-value*	*Significance level*
Less than 30	11	4.8 182	.404 52	F test - 7.520 df - 3	.000
30- 35	51	4.0 196	.882 95		
35- 40	25	4.7 600	.597 22		
More than 40	14	4.4 286	.513 55		
Grand Total	101	4.3 465	.805 43		

Table-5 shows the motive of women entrepreneurs to have their own work-style and life-style and its importance among women entrepreneurs of different age-groups. The overall mean (4.3465) shows that majority of the respondents had preferred to have own work-style and life-style. Women entrepreneurs in the lower age group of 'less than30' considered this factor more important (mean 4.812, SD .40452) as compared to women entrepreneurs in the age group of 'more than 40' years (mean - 4.22 & SD -.5135). The table also shows that young entrepreneurs wanted to have their own work- style and life-style. They wanted more independence. In the age group of '30-35' years mean (.40196) was the lowest and SD (.88295) was the highest as compared to other age groups. Women entrepreneurs in this age group considered this variable important, but they also showed a little disagreement. This disagreement can be because factors like 'security to family' and 'need for money' overcame their need for having own work and life styles. They may be working more out of need than for independence. The F- value (7.520) was found to be statistically significant at 5 per cent level of significance.

In table-6 the motive of women entrepreneurs to earn respect through business profession is depicted. The overall mean value (3.5545) shows that the respondents had considered this factor very important. The age-wise information further shows that women entrepreneurs in the age group of 35-40 years considered this factor more important as compared to those in other age groups. Young women entrepreneurs are more inclined towards achievement. They adopted more risk taking attitude to succeed, and hence are not much concerned about respect. The age group of '35-40' shows the highest mean (3.8400) and the least SD (.62450). This implies that age increases after being entrepreneur for some time, as their business gains stability, the desire for respect becomes important. They wanted to command the respect of the family, friends and society. The age group of 'more than 40' has the lowest mean and the highest SD (1.8156). By this age women entrepreneurs had already earned respect. Therefore 'earning respect' no longer serves as an important motivation factor. The F–value (11.207) is found to be statistically significant at 5 per cent level of significance.

Table - 6: Age and motivational factor 'earn respect'

Age (in years)	*Own work-style and life-style*				
	N	*Mean*	*Std. deviation*	*F-value*	*Significance level*
Less than 30	11	4.8 182	.4045 2	F test - 7.520 df - 3	
30- 35	51	4.0 196	.8829 5		
35- 40	25	4.7 600	.5972 2		.000
More than 40	14	4.4 286	.5135 5		
Grand Total	101	4.3 465	.8054 3		

Table-7 represents the use of decision making skills by women entrepreneurs. The overall mean value (3.8571) suggests that the respondents considered this factor very important for engaging in business. This means that the respondents were confident about their decision making skills. They relied on these skills to engage in business. The members in the lower age groups rated this factor as more important than those in the older age groups. The mean value was the highest for the age group of 'less than 30' and the lowest for more than 40'. This is because younger entrepreneurs are more energetic, confident, and ready to take on challenges. Thc older entrepreneurs also considered this factor very important. Their response was based on their experience. The F-value (3.050) is statistically significant at 5 per cent level of significance.

Table - 7: Age and motivational factor 'decision making skills'

Age (in years)	*Decision making skills*				
	N	*Mean*	*Std. deviation*	*F-value*	*Significance level*
Less than 30	11	4. 2727	1.00 905	F test - 3 .050 df - 3	.033
30- 35	51	3. 9412	1.10 294		
35- 40	25	4. 0800	.70 238		
More than 40	14	3. 8571	1.16 732		
Grand Total	101	4 .00	1.00 995		

Table - 8: Age and motivational factor 'security to family'

Age (in years)	*Provide security to family*				
	N	*Mean*	*Std. deviation*	*F-value*	*Significance level*
Less than 30	11	2.6 364	1. 43337	F test - 1.306 df - 3	.278
30- 35	51	3.5 490	1. 02594		
35- 40	25	3.7 200	1. 02144		
More than 40	14	4.8 571	.3 6314		
Grand Total	101	3.6 733	1. 14986		

In table-8 the motive of women entrepreneurs to provide security to family through business profession is presented. The overall mean (3.673) shows that family security was considered very important. The mean values showed an increasing trend from lower to higher age groups. The SD values show a decreasing trend suggesting that the agreement level was low in the lower age group and high in the higher age group. Younger entrepreneurs considered this factor important and older women considered it extremely important. This is because younger women are ambitious while family responsibilities keep on increasing as the age of women increases, and they want to ensure security and stability in the family through their business. The F-value (1.306) is statistically significant at 5 per cent level of significance.

Table - 9: Age and motivational factor 'to satisfy innovative instinct'

Age (in years)	*To satisfy innovative instinct*				
	N	*Mean*	*Std. deviation*	*F-value*	*Significance level*
Less than 30	11	4. 8182	.40 452		
30- 35	51	4. 2549	.86 817	F test -	
35- 40	25	4 .200	.86 603	1.741	.166
More than 40	14	3. 4286	1.2 225	df - 3	
Grand Total	101	4. 1881	.945 65		

Table-9 shows the distribution of women entrepreneurs of different age groups regarding their motive to satisfy innovative instinct by engaging in business. The factor is considered extremely important as suggested by overall mean value (4.188). The age-wise information further shows that as age increased the mean values had decreased. This is because younger women are more innovative. They are more enthusiastic about using new methods and techniques, and are not afraid of experimenting. They engage in business to make use of their education, talents and skills and achieve satisfaction. Majority of women had agreed that they wanted to work to satisfy their innovative instincts. As the age increased the women preferred stability in business. The F-value (1.741) is statistically significant at 5 per cent level of significance.

The motive of women entrepreneurs to have more earnings through business profession is presented in table-10. The overall mean value (4.3663) shows that this motivating factor was extremely important for women of all age groups. The factor was of greater importance for women in lower age groups as compared to women in higher age groups. The young entrepreneurs belonging to the age group of less than 30 years showed a high level of agreement for this factor. Young entrepreneurs have a strong desire for extra earnings, more pocket money, and a high level of energy and ambition. The older women preferred respect and status to earnings. But the mean value of the age group of 'more than 40' (4.7143) shows that desire for extra earnings remained an extremely important factor. The respondents seemed to enjoy the extra earnings. They wanted it for security and for maintaining status and expensive life-style. The F-value (4.228) is statistically significant at 5 per cent level of significance.

Table - 10: Age and motivational factor 'Desire for more earnings'

Age (in years)	*Desire for more earnings*				
	N	*Mean*	*Std. deviation*	*F-value*	*Significance level*
Less than 30	11	5.0000	.0000	F test - 4.228 df - 3	.008
30- 35	51	4.1961	.60065		
35- 40	25	4.2400	.77889		
More than 40	14	4.7143	.72627		
Grand Total	101	4.3663	.68881		

Table - 11: Age and motivational factor 'To be your own boss'

Age (in years)	*To be your own boss*				
	N	*Mean*	*Std. deviation*	*F-value*	*Significance level*
Less than 30	11	4.7273	.46710	F test - df - 3	.000
30- 35	51	3.5294	.83314		
35- 40	25	3.6800	1.06927		
More than 40	14	4.1429	.86444		
Grand Total	101	3.7822	.94450		

Table-11 shows the variation among the women entrepreneurs in different age groups regarding their motive to be their own boss. The overall mean value (3.7822) shows that the motive to be own boss was very important. The factor was of extreme importance for women entrepreneurs in the low and old age groups as compared to those in the middle age groups. Respondents belonging to the age group of less than 30 years considered this factor extremely important. They preferred independence in work and life. They wanted to make their own decisions, to learn through challenges and were more adventurous.

The older women did not like taking orders at their age. They wanted to order, direct, manage, nurture people younger than them. They wanted to be respected for their experience. Thus they also rated this factor as extremely important (mean value 4.142 in age group 'more than 40'). Women entrepreneurs belonging to middle age groups, i.e., 30-35 years and 35-40 years considered this factor very important. They also wanted independence in respect of their work. They also worked to satisfy their need to control others through business, which might not have been possible at home where the male would be dominant. The F-value is statistically significant at 5 per cent level of significance.

Conclusion

Entrepreneurship ensures a promising future for women. It allows them to have control over themselves and provides flexibility to their life. As the study was conducted in the NCR region a huge diversity was found regarding the nature of businesses of women entrepreneurs. It is high time to realise that significant contribution is being made by women entrepreneurs towards social and economic development and this contribution goes on increasing with passing time. This potential of women entrepreneurs, whether rural or urban, is waiting to be unleashed. The growth of women entrepreneurs should be looked upon from the perspective of family, state and national development. Various successful schemes need to be suitably modified to cater to the local demand. Entrepreneurial activities from home should be equally encouraged because women have to nurture the younger minds at home who could become future entrepreneurs. This will help them manage both their business and the household chores. Through entrepreneurship, substantial changes can be brought about in the socio-economic conditions of women by providing gainful employment opportunities.

6

Street Entrepreneurship Among Tribal Women: Insights from Mizoram

Rodi Lalremruati
Rama Ramswamy

Abstract

Women entrepreneurs play a significant role in the street markets of the tribal state of Mizoram. Street entrepreneurship has always been subsumed under the realm of informal economy and, till recent times, ignored and disdained. However, in refutation of the early views on informal entrepreneurship as simply a residue or leftover from an earlier mode of production and as a disappearing phenomenon, research studies in recent times have depicted them as entrepreneurs possessing entrepreneurial attributes, traits and qualities This paper is based on a study conducted in Thakthing street market, in Aizawl where about 450 street entreprenurs sell vegetables in the Saturday 'Zing' Bazaar. Entrepreneurship is largely a socio-economic phenomenon, as entrepreneurs are embedded in socio economic systems such as caste, education, religion, income, age, which mould their entrepreneurial attitudes. This paper attempts to study the social framework of the entrepreneurs, viz. tribal origin, religion, caste, gender, family structure, family size, educational qualifications and marital status of the street entrepreneurs in Thakthing market.

Introduction

Local street markets play a crucial role in livelihood security and are at the epicenter of local commerce. Street vending as a profession has been in existence in India since times immemorial. Street entrepreneurship has always been subsumed under the realm of informal economy and, till recent times, ignored and disdained.

However, in refutation of the early views on informal entrepreneurs as simply a residue or leftover from an earlier mode of production and as a disappearing phenomenon, research studies in recent times have depicted them as entrepreneurs possessing entrepreneurial attributes, traits and qualities (ILO 2002; Small Business Council 2004; Venkatesh 2006; Volkov 2002; Webb et al. 2009; Williams 2006; Williams and Round 2007). They should no more be considered as being at the fringe of society.

India today presents a picture of contrasts where a majority of her population is living on low incomes and has low quality of life. According to the Human Development Report (HRD) of the United Nations Development Programme (UNDP 2013), India ranks 136th among 186 countries in the Human Development Index (HDI). The HDI is a comparative measure of life expectancy, literacy, education and standard of living of 186 countries worldwide. Further, the fact that India has also scored a low rank (101 among 136 countries) in the Global Gender Gap Report (World Economic Forum 2013) is particularly of great concern. The Global Gender Gap Index examines the gap between men and women in four fundamental categories: economic participation and opportunity, educational attainment, political empowerment, and health and survival. It is distressing to note that India is far behind even her neighbour Bangladesh, which ranks 75th in the Report.

In this context, 'inclusive growth', which brings into its ambit the development of people at large especially under-privileged sections of population such as women, Scheduled Castes (SCs), Scheduled Tribes (STs) and other backward communities (OBC) assumes significance.

It is widely recognised today that the informal sector is an expanding feature of the contemporary global economy (Williams and Gurtoo 2011). It is estimated that out of a global working population of about 3 billion, nearly two-thirds (1.8 billion) are informal workers (Jutting and Laiglesia 2009). According to the ILO (2002), the informal sector accounts for 93 per cent of the total work-force in India. Moreover, in all developing regions, self-employment comprises a greater share of informal employment (outside agriculture) than wage employment, specifically; self- employment represents 70 per cent of informal employment in sub-Saharan Africa, 62 per cent in North Africa, 60 per cent in Latin America and 59 per cent in Asia. The self-employed constitute 52 per cent of non-agricultural informal employment in India (ILO 2002).

Notably, one-third of the work-force in India's informal sector is comprised of women, and these women contributed to 20 per cent of the GDP of India (National Sample Survey Organisation 2005). It is evident that the informal entrepreneurs are, hence, not at the fringe of the economy but, in fact, play a significant role in inclusive development of the Indian economy.

In this backdrop, it is important to transcend the demarcated boundary of 'formal' and 'informal' and find ways to allow 'space' for the development of informal entrepreneurs. According to Cross and Morales (2007), policy makers should create ways in which these systems (distinct) can intersect while existing side by side.

Street entrepreneurship: conceptual framework

Street vending is one of the world's oldest and most widespread occupations. In fact street vendors are one of the largest sub-groups of the informal workforce (ILO 2002). Cross and Karides (2007), observed that though the micro-businesses operated by street vendors are struggling, they are not at the fringe of the society. Rather, street vendors not only participate in commercial exchange and urban politics, but also shape the spatial organisation of cities.

Researchers have found that street vending, despite the problems it faces, is a growing phenomenon in both developed and developing economies. According to Cross and Morales (2007), street vending minimises overhead costs of rent and utilities is ideally suited for low-skilled employment and fits with a new ideology of independence and entrepreneurship.

Street entrepreneur has been defined as a person who offers goods for sale to the public at large without having a permanent built-up structure from which to sell. Street vendors may be stationary in the sense that they occupy space on the pavements or other public/private spaces or they may be mobile (Bhowmik 2007). According to Kathleen Staudt (2007) street vendors use public space for commerce and trade. The cost of doing business and the credentials for their work are minimal. They require mainly people skills and math. Many people can do this sort of income generating work without degrees and a large amount of capital.

There has been a considerable increase in the number of street vendors across the globe. Bhowmik (2005) observed an increase of street vendors in the cities of Thailand, Singapore, Philippines, Bangladesh, Malaysia, Sri Lanka, Cambodia, South Korea and India. The National Policy on Urban Street Vendors/ Hawkers estimated that the street vendors constitute about 2 per cent of the population of a metropolis in India. With a total population of about 10 million, Dhaka, the capital city of Bangladesh has around 90,000 street vendors, Colombo (Sri Lanka) has 8,000 - 10,000; Bangkok (Thailand) has 20,000; Singapore, 50,000, Kuala Lumpur 35,000 (Malaysia), Manila (Phillipines) 15,000 and in Seoul (South Korea) 8,00,000 (Bhowmik 2005).

The number of street entreprenurs in India has also increased manifold in recent decades. According to the 'National Policy on Urban Street Vendors', Mumbai has the largest number of street vendors numbering around 2,50,000. While Delhi has around 2,00,000, Kolkata has more than 1,50,000 and Ahmedabad around 1,00,000 street vendors (Bhowmik 2000). In most of the Indian cities, the urban poor survive by working in the formal sector. Poverty and lack of employment in the rural areas and smaller towns drive large numbers of people to the cities for work (Bhowmik 2007).

Street entrepreneurs in north-east India

There is a dearth of research on informal entrepreneurs in the North-Eastern states of India. A few significant works were conducted in Nagaland, Manipur and Guwahati.

Vengotanakro and Chozule (2006) conducted a study on women vegetable vendors in four villages in Nagaland namely Khonoma, Tsiese, Basa, Merema and Pholami, and suggested better implementation of policy and development plans for tribal women.

The National Alliance of Street Vendors in India (NASVI) had organised a study in the year 2k on hawkers in seven Indian cities including Imphal (Manipur). It was observed that in Imphal all the street vendors were women and they had gained some legal rights. Imphal is perhaps the only city which clearly states the rules for street trading. The Manipur Town Planning and Country Planning Act, 1975 provides that in residential areas (which include private as well as government housing) there should be provisions for 4 to 6 shops and 10 hawkers per 1,000 people (Bhowmik 2005).

A study conducted in Guwahati highlighted the contribution of street vendors in providing cheap food to people and the employment potential. It was also noted that the vendors faced the problem of capital. They depended mainly on loans from friends, family or money lenders to run their business. Even those that are licensed rarely approach banks because of the huge paper work involved (Bhattacharya as cited in Bhowmik 2005).

The *Zing* Bazaar of Mizoram: Thakthing

The Saturday street market in Mizoram is popularly known as the 'Zing Bazaar.'The history of the Thakthing Zing Bazaar can be traced to the early 1980s when around 20 street vendors sold vegetables on the pavements of the road from Sikulpuikawn to Thakthing Tlang. All kinds of products from clothes, toiletries, household electrical appliances, footwear, vegetables, fruits, cereals, etc., are sold on the pavements by street vendors. A few Manipuri street vendors are also seen selling cooked food products. The market is dominated by woman entrepreneurs, often seen with their minor children. The word 'Thakthing' means Cinnamon, denoting that cinnamon was widely grown in this hill. They lay their products for sale on the pavement in the designated place from the early hours on Saturdays. Vendors from far flung villages arrive in the market on Friday night and stay on the pavements often with their minor children.

The customers start streaming in from the wee hours of Saturday morning. The peak hours of the market are from 7 – 11am when the street becomes crowded with customers. The street from Thakthing to Thakthing Tlang is closed for vehicular traffic from the early hours of Saturday to 6:30pm. About 450 entrepreneurs sell vegetables in the Zing Bazaar. They sustain their Saturday market day on cereals and cups of tea sold in the market. They mainly converse in the Mizo language, but the occasional 'Non Mizo' customer manages to communicate with them in broken Hindi or by gestures. They sell mainly fresh vegetables both seasonal and non-seasonal and; onions, garlic, potatoes and spices.

Objective and methodology

This paper has attempted to examine the socio-cultural origins and characteristics of tribal street entrepreneurs in Aizawl.

The present study covers the Thakthing market street, located in the southern part of Aizawl city, which extends from Kulikawn to Sikulpuikawn on Saturdays. The vegetable vending by street entrepreneurs operating on Thakthing street market (without permanent built-up structures for selling vegetables) on Saturdays was studied. The study is based mainly on primary data collected through field research by administering a structured questionnaire/schedule (based on formula developed by Krejcie and Morgan, 1970), to a sample of 196 entrepreneurs (out of about 450 entrepreneurs selling vegetables in the street market of Thakthing on Saturdays) during February to July 2012.

Discussion

Social framework of the entrepreneurs' community

The socio-economic milieu plays an important role in the emergence and development of entrepreneurship. In fact, entrepreneurship is largely a socio–economic phenomenon as entrepreneurs are embedded in socio-economic systems such as caste, income, age and parental occupation which mould their entrepreneurial attitudes. Cross and Morales (2007), observed that street entrepreneurs earn income, but they do so within the boundaries of complex social and household dynamics.

Although much research has been conducted on various facets of entrepreneurship there is a dearth of academic research on street entrepreneurship in tribal areas of the country which are represented by sociological variables that capture the nature of livelihood systems of Scheduled tribes. Vendors and their ability to adjust to local stressors are not emphasised in community assessment (Companion 2007). A study of the socio- economic environment of street entrepreneurs in Thakthing may provide a clue to the emergence of street entrepreneurship in tribal areas in the North- East.

Williams and Gurtoo (2011) in their study on women entrepreneurs in India exemplify the informal entrepreneurs' trait of willingness to engage with the socio-cultural and economic factors of working in the informal economy. They averred that conceptualisation of street entrepreneurs must transcend the typical definition that highlights entrepreneurship as merely possessing motivational traits to the concept of willingness to operate in a unique and challenging socio-economic spectrum.

The main objective of this section is to study the socio-cultural characteristics viz. tribal origin, religion, caste, gender, family structure, family size, educational qualifications and marital status of the street entrepreneurs in Thakthing street market only.

The 'Zing Bazaar' in Thakthing has the highest percentage of the street vegetable vendors in the whole state of Mizoram. The present study covers the vegetable vending street entrepreneurs operating on Thakthing street market located in the southern part of Aizawl city. They have no permanent facility for selling vegetables.

Religion and caste of entrepreneurs

Setty (2002) observed that in tribal societies, the family is bound by the kin group with a set of consanguineous and affinal kin, shaping and influencing the individuals' decision making and behaviour. Most of the respondents in the present study belonged to the Mizo community. A few entrepreneurs from the neighbouring country

Myanmar and neighbouring state of Manipur were also observed among the street vendors. All the entrepreneurs from Mizoram belonged to the Scheduled Tribe category.

All the entrepreneurs in the present study were Christians. Cohen and Tinker (1985), in their study on women entrepreneurship in West Africa, observed that religious beliefs have a strong influence on the operation of woman enterprises in the informal sector. According to them, religious, cultural and traditional values and prejudices are key determinants to the success of woman enterprises. In particular, Cohen (2000) further observed that religious beliefs set the boundaries within which street food vendors operated in Tunisia, Bangladesh and Egypt. A similar study (Otoo et al 2010) on women entrepreneurs in the street food sector in West Africa observed that religion played a significant role in determining the operation and success of enterprises. They observed that Christian entrepreneurs were more successful than Muslim entrepreneurs who observed seclusion in Kumasi, Ghana.

Social relationships are not dominated by caste dimensions in the Mizo community as observed in most parts of India. The Mizo community comprises of different tribes, sub- tribes and their clans. Mizos adopted and practised heredity chieftainship in pre- Independent India, which was later changed to a system of administration introduced by the British. The Christianity brought by the British missionaries illuminated the political, economical, socio-cultural and especially living trends of the Mizo society.

The State of Mizoram is inhabited by a number of tribes which may be broadly divided into nine major and 13 minor tribes and sub-tribes (Verghese & Thanzawna 1997). These tribes and sub-tribes are further divided into a number of clans. The major tribes of Mizoram are: Lushai or Lusei, Pawi or Lai, Hmar, Lakher or Mara, Paihte, Ralte, Chakma, Riang or Tuikuk. The sub-tribes are Chawngthu, Ngente, Khawlhring, Khiangte, Pautu, Rawite, Renthlei, Tlau, Vangchhia, Zawngte, Pang and Bawng. The Lusei consists of 10 commoner and six chief clans. The commoner clans include Pachuau, Chhangte, Chawhte, Hauhnar, Chuango, Hrahsel, Tochhawng, Vanchhawng and Chhakchhuak and the six Chief clans are Zadeng, Palian, Rokhum, Sailo, Thangluah, Rivung.

Table-1 gives the details of the different tribes/clans/ sub-clans of the respondents in the study.As indicated by the table, thirty-nine different types/clans were involved in the study of entrepreneurship among vegetable street vendors including the chief clans such as Sailo, Zadeng and others which are traditionally represented by the chief of the tribe. Fanai is the largest tribe represented among the entrepreneurs (15.31 %) followed by Chawhte clan (12.76%) which is again followed by the Sailo clan (7.14 %). It was observed that out of 196 sample entrepreneurs, three persons belonged to Gurkhali community of Nepal.

Gender and street entrepreneurship

Women play a significant role in the informal sector particularly in the third world countries. However, it was rightly observed by UNDP (1993) that their contribution often goes unnoticed, undocumented or is just ignored. UNIDO (2001) observed that womens' entrepreneurial activities, whether in the informal or formal sector, are not only the means for their economic survival but also has positive repercussions for themselves and their environment. Entrepreneurship represents an appropriate opportunity for women all over the world as it is flexible for entry, change and innovation.

Table - 1: Distribution of tribes/sub-tribes/clans of entrepreneurs

Sl.No	*Clans*	*Number*	*Percentage*
1.	Baw itl ung	2	1.02
2.	Baw lte	2	1.02
3.	Boitlung	13	6.63
4.	Chawhte	25	12.76
5.	Chawngthu	1	0.51
6.	Chhak chhuak	11	5.61
7.	Chhangte	7	3.57
8.	Chhunthang	1	0.51
9.	Chinzah	9	4.59
10.	Fanai	30	15.31
11.	Fanchun	9	4.59
12.	Guite	12	6.12
13.	Hauhnar	5	2.55

(Contd...)

14.	Hlawndo	13	6.63
15.	Hmar	1	0.51
16.	Hnamte	2	1.02
17.	Hrahse l	2	1.02
18.	Kaw ilam	1	0.51
19.	Kaw lni	4	2.04
20.	Khawl hring	1	0.51
21.	Khi angte	1	0.51
22.	Lai	2	1.02
23.	Nge nte	2	1.02
24.	Pachuau	2	1.02
25.	Paite	1	0.51
26.	Pautu	1	0.51
27.	Ralte	2	1.02
28.	Re nthl ei	2	1.02
29.	Sai lo	14	7.14
30.	Tlau	3	1.53
31.	Tochhaw ng	1	0.51
32.	Vangchhia	3	1.53
33.	Varte	1	0.51
34.	Vuite	1	0.51
35.	Zadeng	1	0.51
36.	Zahau	2	1.02
37.	Zote	1	0.51
38.	Jo ngte	2	1.02
	Total	193	100.00

Street entrepreneurship has attracted marginalised women as an income earning activity world over. According to the National Sample Survey Organisation (2005), women comprise about one-third of the sizeable informal work-force in India and contribute 20 per cent to the GDP of India. According to the ILO (2002), women also play a significant role in street vending in the developing countries. Several studies conducted in Bangladesh (Qaiz 2000), Sri Lanka (Bhowmik 2005), Cambodia (Francesca and Moller 2003, and Kyoko 2003), Seoul (Noritake 2008), Lima, Peru (Herrera et al. 2012), African cities, Lyon (2007), Otoo et al (2010), Hugon and Hugon (1989), Herrera et al. (2012), Budlender (2011), and in cities in India (Bhatt 2006; Carr and Chen 2002; Mehotra and Biggeri 2002; Williams and Gurtoo 2011) have shed light on the significance of the role women play in street entrepreneurial activities. Cohen et al (2000) examined the experience of women working and organising as urban street vendors. It explored how economically marginalised women are pursuing income generating activities amidst growing global competition for access to markets, low cost commodities and low wage, workers.

Interestingly, studies conducted in some NE states in India identified the predominance of women in street entrepreneurial activities. In a study conducted in Manipur (Bhowmik 2007) all the street entrepreneurs were found to be women.Astudy conducted in Nagaland in four villages (Vegotanakro and Chozhule 2006) underlined the importance of women entrepreneurs in the vegetable vending business activities in Nagaland.

The present study enquired into the gender composition of the street entrepreneurs operating in Thakthing street market. This market presents a similar picture with 95.41 per cent of the entrepreneurs studied being women. Table-2 shows that out of 196 street entrepreneurs interviewed 187, were women.

Table - 2: Gender of entrepreneurs

Gender	No. of entrepreneurs	Percentage
Female	187	95.41
Male	9	4.59
Total	196	100

It is evident that street entrepreneurship offers income earning opportunities to the marginalised tribal women in the capital city of Aizawl. This speaks of the predominance of woman entrepreneurs in street vending in Aizawl. It is a common sight to find women predominantly conducting business activities in Mizoram. The shops, bazaars and markets in Aizawl are full of woman sellers.

Education

The researchers have further probed into the educational background of the entrepreneurs to understand the social factors that determined the entry of these women into street entrepreneurship.

According to the Census Report 2011, Mizoram ranks among the top states in terms of literacy with a literacy rate of about 91.6 per cent, which is much above the national average of 74.04 per cent.

Though research evidence (Ayadurai 2004; Ostgard and Birly 1996) has associated higher levels of education with greater success of any business, Honig (1998) argued that for street food enterprises, basic literacy and numeracy are sufficient for day-to-day operation. Otoo et al. (2010) also contradicted this literature and concluded that higher educational levels are not necessarily associated with more successful enterprises in the case of street food entrepreneurs.

Literature on street entrepreneurship reveals that street entrepreneurs have low levels of education. In fact, this is a significant 'push' factor that very often compels them into this form of economic activity as the last option as lack of higher education restrains their entry into formal sector jobs.

Bhowmik (2007) observed that in most of the Indian cities, the urban poor survive by working in the informal sector. Poverty and lack of employment in the rural areas and smaller towns drive large numbers of people to the cities for work. These people generally possess low skills and lack the education required for better-paid jobs in the formal sector. In fact, permanent protected jobs in the formal sector are declining; hence even those having the requisite skills are often unable to find proper employment. For these people, work in the informal sector is the only means for survival. Street vending is an important option for these people, as it requires small financial input and basic skills, though the income is low. However, street vending has been systematically ignored by academicians and considered as a nuisance by policy makers.

Table - 3: Entrepreneurs education level

Education	*No. entrepreneurs*	*Percentage*
Illiterate	20	10.20
Primary school	98	50.00
Secondary school	58	29.59
College degree	17	8.67
Any other	3	1.53
Total	196	100

Table-3 shows that among the entrepreneurs, illiterates comprise 10.20 per cent those who attended primary school formed 50 per cent, secondary school 29.59 per cent and the vendors who attended college were 8.67 per cent. It shows that most of the street entrepreneurs do not have higher levels of education. This finding conforms to the results of several studies conducted in other cities in India, Bangladesh, Nepal, Cambodia, Vietnam and African countries where the educational levels of street entrepreneurs were found to be low.

Otoo et al.'s (2010) study on street entrepreneurs in West Africa observed that self- employment in the informal sector was the sole option for African women having low education.

Bhowmik (2007) observed that street entrepreneurs generally possess low skills and lack the level of education for better paid jobs in the formal sector. A similar study conducted (Otunga et al 1998) on 304 women street entrepreneurs engaged mainly in the sale of vegetables, fruits, fish, seasonings and other agricultural produce in Eldoret, Kenya observed that 10 per cent of the respondents were illiterate, about 50 per cent had only primary education and about 40 per cent had secondary level education. They observed that these levels of education provided the basic skills of communication and numeracy in both English and the local language - *Kiswahilu*. Almost all the entrepreneurs perceived that this education helped them in socialisations and communication, giving correct change and predicting the business environment. Research studies conducted in Phnom Penh (Kyoko 2003), India, Bangladesh, Nepal, Cambodia (Bhowmik 2005) and Vietnam (Tantiwaramond, as cited in Bhowmik 2005) also noted that most of the street entrepreneurs had low levels of education.

Noritake (2008), in her study conducted in Seoul, observed that street business created opportunities for those with low educational qualification and limited access to capital. Lack of gainful employment coupled with poverty and low levels of education force them to settle for self-employment in informal sector. Tantiwaramond's study also observed that low levels of education among street entrepreneurs in Hanoi impeded their employment opportunities in the formal sector and forced them to take up street vending as a means of survival.

The entrepreneurs in Thakthing '*Zing*' bazaar conversed in the local Mizo language and were very articulate in their communication with the customers. They were not fluent with the national language 'Hindi' but managed to communicate the price by gesturing with their fingers to the rare non-local customer who could not converse in Mizo language.

Age of entrepreneurs

Age of the entrepreneurs is shown in table-4.

Table - 4: Age of the entrepreneurs

Age	*Year*	*Percentage*
Below 30	23	11.73
Between 31 – 40	89	45.41
Between 41 – 50	55	28.06
Between 51 – 60	17	8.67
More than 60	12	6.12
	196	100.00

From the table, it can be observed that women in the age bracket of below 30 years constituted only 11.73 per cent, while 73.47 per cent of women were in the age group of 30-50 years. Fewer woman entrepreneurs were beyond the age of 51 years. It appears that this business does not attract young persons below the age of 30 years. An enquiry into the marital status also revealed that unmarried girls do not prefer this business. Interestingly, only 6 per cent of the entrepreneurs beyond 60 years of age were found to be engaged in street businesses.

Marital status of the entrepreneurs

Marital status of the entrepreneurs has been enquired into, to understand the support and encouragement provided by the family to the entrepreneurs. Table-5 shows the marital status of the sample street entrepreneurs in Aizawl.

Table-5 shows that married people formed the largest segment with 63.78 per cent among the 196 sample. Divorced or separated comprised 16.33 per cent and the widowed 11.22 per cent. Interestingly, only 8.67 per cent of entrepreneurs were single. It appears that the business is dominated by married women.

Table - 5: Entrepreneurs' marital status

Marital status	*No. of entrepreneurs*	*Percentage*
Unmarried	17	8.67
Married	125	63.78
Divorced or separated	32	16.33
Widowed	22	11.22
	196	100

Almost all the married women were augmenting the income of the family by street entrepreneurship. Moreover, their entry into street entrepreneurship may be attributed to support from the spouse. Lalrinawma (2005) in his study observed that it is common in many of the families in Mizoram that married women contribute to the family income, and in some cases they are the sole contributors.

A similar study (Otunga et al, 1998), in Eldoret, Kenya shows that about 25 per cent of the entrepreneurs were single (un-married) and about 45 per cent were married.

It appears that single women abstain from engaging in street business in Takhthing. Street entrepreneurship also seems to support a large number of divorced and widowed women (27.5% of respondents).

Family structure and size

Traditionally, the Indian society followed the joint family system, but as a consequence of growing industrialisation and urbanisation joint family system is slowly disintegrating, giving way to independent family system.

Lalrinawma (2005) observed that joint family system was still prevailing in Mizoram. This is also evident in the present study, that a high proportion (85.20%) of the entrepreneurs in Thakthing were living in joint families. Only 14.80 per cent of the entrepreneurs were living in nucleus families. Table-6 shows the family size of the entrepreneurs.

Table - 6: Entrepreneurs' family size

Family size	*No. of entrepreneurs*	*Percentage*
Upto 5	99	50.51
6 to 10	90	45.92
11 to 15	6	3.06
Above 15	1	0.51
Total	196	100

It may be observed that 50.51 per cent of the entrepreneurs belonged to families of up to five members, 45.92 per cent to families of 6-10 members, 3.06 per cent were from families of 11-15 members, and 0.15 per cent of entrepreneurs had come from families of above 15 members. Notably, though joint family system dominantly prevailed among the sample entrepreneurs, the size is mostly restricted to less than 10 members.

Conclusion

In conclusion, Thakthing Zing bazaar plays a central role in livelihood security. It is at the epicenter of local commerce and has become a hub of information exchange and socialisation, and is embedded in socio-cultural tribal systems. It should no more be considered as at the fringe of society.

The market comprises predominantly of tribal women selling their wares on the busy street of the city. Women entrepreneurs were playing a dominant role in the Zing bazaar comprising 95.41 per cent of the respondents. Though the literacy rates were high (90%), 50 per cent of the respondents attained only primary level of education, about 30 per cent had completed secondary education and only 8 per cent possessed college degree. Majority of the entrepreneurs were in the age bracket of 31-40 years and joint family system dominated the family structure of 85.20 per cent of entrepreneurs. Interestingly, the present study observed that street entrepreneurship is an important avenue for women with low educational qualifications. In the absence of gainful employment in the formal sector, this form of business activity has significant implications for poverty alleviation among the under-privileged tribal women in Mizoram.

7

Women's Decision Making and Mobility in Carpet Industry: Study of Bhadohi District

Heena Saudagar
Zeeshan
Shreekant Sharma

Abstract

The relationship between development and gender empowerment remains unclear, especially in small scale industries like carpet industry where industrial growth has not brought about any noticeable change in gender relations. This paper attempts to find out the condition of women working in the carpet industry of Bhadohi. A Decision Making Index has been formed to measure the empowerment level of adult females engaged in the carpet industry. To measure the empowerment of women through decision making, socio-economic as well as demographic factors have been included. The decision-making index has been developed by summing up the feedback of the respondents through the descriptive statistics and regression analysis. The survey proves that most of the adult females in the carpet industry have a low degree of decision making. The decision making index showed that 58 per cent of adult females exhibited low decision making, 30 per cent had medium level and only 12 per cent of adult females in the carpet industry had high decision making index. This reflects the poor empowerment of women laborers in the carpet industry of Bhadohi. Findings from cross-sectional data showed that placement of work, their working experience, the headship of the family, the right to spend and wages had an empowering force.

Keywords: *Decisions Making Index, carpet industry, multiple linear regression analysis*

Introduction

Economic growth and development can be accelerated by tapping the unleashed potential of the female work-force by giving them equal opportunity and resources. Thus, women's participation can become an important element in the process of growth and development. No society can develop leaving behind their women. Women constitute 48.46 per cent of the Indian population (census 2011). Development becomes impossible when almost 50 per cent of the population is left behind. Participation of women is essential for the development and growth of the country as it leads to an increase in the human resource, both quantitatively as well as qualitatively. The child sex ratio is skewed in favour of men; the literacy rate is low among women as compared to men. This clearly shows the poor condition of women in the Indian scenario. Development requires the participation of both sexes with equality and justice. Women empowerment has been defined by many in several ways. Empowerment can be said to give power or to make an investment in power (Bathliwala 1995). According to the UN, women empowerment has five major components: women's sense of self-worth; the right to have and to determine choices; right to have access to opportunities and resources; right to have the power to control their own lives, both within and outside home; ability to influence the direction of social change to create better social and economic order, nationally and internationally.

The UNDP has also recognised the importance of women empowerment and deemed that development is impossible if women are not included in the process of development. Thus, UNDP incorporated two gender-based measures which are Gender Development Index (GDI) and Gender Empowerment Measure (GEM). Women empowerment is being actively promoted these days. Promotion of gender equality has been one among the eight Millennium Development Goals (MDG UNFPA 2005). Most of the national and international agencies have recognised five basic indicators of women empowerment: economic contribution, education, governance, health status and media exposure (Chung et al. 2013).

Human development in India is very low, as also the condition of women, ranking 130 in Gender Inequality Index as well as in human development index (Human Development Report 2015). Only through education and employment, women can be empowered (Nayak and Mahanta 2009). The word 'empowerment' means not income earning alone but also having command over one's life. The capability theory of Amartya Sen fits the women empowerment scenario also. Women will be empowered only if they are made capable and have command over their life and decision making. Women's decision making power has a great influence on the well- being of children, especially the girl-child (Smith and Byron 2005). Therefore women decision making in household matters should be given a wider space as this will lead to improvement of her life as well as of the whole family.

The female work participation rate in India is very low, as the recent census (2011) has revealed. The female work-force participation is 25.51 per cent, whereas for males it is 53.26 per cent. The rural-urban differential is also quite high when it comes to female work-force participation rate. The rural females are ahead of urban females when it comes to female work-force participation with 30.02 per cent as against and 15.44 per cent for urban females. The reason for higher rural female work participation is due to poverty as well as the nature of work done by women in rural areas. The lower urban female labour participation is due to the difference in educational status and job position between men and women. This signifies that women whose husbands earn more, are less likely to work. As a whole, female work participation is as low as 25.5 per cent. The reasons may be the cultural and social discrimination against women. Empowerment can be measured by the level of command over life and decision making. Women might earn but might not have command over their earnings as well as over their life. Women's decision to earn also rests mostly with the husband (Sen et al. 2006). The condition of women is poor in India from both educational and employment perspectives (Baro and Sarania 2014).

The study pertains to women in the carpet industry in Bhadohi district. Though area-wise the place is tiny, its contribution to hand-made carpets is huge. This area is called the carpet belt of the nation along with Mirzapur, which is also very small. Bhadohi is one of the smallest districts of Uttar Pradesh, where the prime occupation of the people is carpet making. The district is surrounded by Jaunpur district to the north, Varanasi district to the east, Mirzapur district to the south, and Allahabad district to the west.

The industry is labour-intensive and thus the most important element is labour. This labour constitutes both men and women. But women labourers remain a neglected part of the system. Importance is not given to them in their household itself. The women in the carpet industry are contributing to their household, yet their contribution goes unrecognised and does not impact their status. The study has, therefore, made an attempt to find out the empowerment level of women who work in the carpet industry of Bhadohi in their household.

Review of literature

Studies have been conducted by different researchers on this subject. They tried to measure women's condition in a different set-up. Afew are listed below.

Sharma et al., (2013) in his study made an attempt to find out the decision- makingpower of women in relation to farm activities of Jammu. The Decision- Making Index (DMI) was evolved through constructing the questionnaire and schedule and finding out the involvement. It was divided into nil, partial and full involvement of women in the decision-making. The study found that the involvement of women was meagre and almost in all the decisions men or the husband/head of household decided the matters.

Sheikh and Sadaqat (2015) made an attempt to find out the level of empowerment of women in Pakistan. They used a similar measure by constructing an economic empowerment index (EEI) of women in Pakistan. The study showed that only 8 per cent of women had high EEI while 36 per cent had low economic empowerment and 56 per cent were moderately empowered. Marital status, household size, family system, headship of household by husband and purdah system had a negative effect on the empowerment of women. However, the age of women, education, working status, income, access to micro credit, ownership of property, father's education, family's bank account, savings, physical assets, place of residence and media exposure have increased the level of empowerment of women in Pakistan.

Parveen and Leonhauser (2004) conducted a study in Bangladesh which showed the poor condition of women. A cumulative empowerment index (CEI) was constructed which revealed that around 82 per cent of women had a very low or moderate empowerment. Their study showed that education, exposure to media and information increased the empowerment of women, while traditional and socio-cultural norms reduced the CEI of women.

Sen et al. (2006) showed that in many cases of household decision making, generation plays more dominant role than gender. Senior members of the family, especially senior women create more hurdles in the decision making of younger women. The decision making power among women can be affected by age factor significantly.

Masood and Ahmad (2009) argued that the rural female work-force participation, though high when compared to urban female work-force participation, showed no positive relationship between education, wages, and female work-force participation. This is mainly due to poverty constraints: women work to feed themselves and their children.

A look at the studies relating to women empowerment has made it possible to find the scope for study in a new direction. The studies undertaken earlier focused on either decision making criteria or economic empowerment criteria. In this study, an attempt has been made to cover both aspects, but thefocus remains on the economic empowerment issue. Variables such as thelocation of work also affect the empowerment level of women, which was not taken into account in previous studies. Thus, many new variables have been included which were not considered by previous studies.

Data and methodology

The study seeks to examine the socio-economic factors which determine women's participation in decision-making in thehousehold and economic activities of women engaged in thecarpet industry. The paper is based on primary field study done in March-April, 2017 in the Bhadohi district of Uttar Pradesh. A multi-stage random sampling design was used for the selection of the sample women. In the first stage, Bhadohi was selected purposely keeping the high production in mind. In the second stage, two blocks namely Bhadohi and Aurai were purposely selected from the district by the same criterion. In the third stage, two villages namely Rayan and Auraihave been randomly selected from the selected blocks. In the final stage 25 women who engaged in carpet industry were randomly selected for the field survey from each area. Thus, the total sample consists of 50 women. The Bhadohi region has been selected, as it contributes highest percentage share in carpet production in India and at the same time this region has the highest share in carpet exports as well.

Information from the selected women was collected with the help of structured survey schedule. Data on various aspects of socio-economic conditions of households and other related dimensions was collected and processed using the MS- EXCELand STATA packages. Multiple regression analysis has been used to examine the determinants of female participation in household decisions.

The study is divided into two parts. First, an attempt has been made to find out the economic empowerment index of women. This index has been constructed through measuring the level of decision making of women. Once the Decision-Making Index (DMI) has been found, the next step is to examine the determinants of Decision Making Index (DMI) by applying Multiple Regression Analysis Technique.

The Index covers 24 types of activities on which women were asked to indicate the extent of their participation in decision making. Women with no participation in the decision-making were given one score. Ascore of two was given if women were only informed about thedecision. Ascore of three was given if women's opinion was given some weight. Ascore of four was given if women participated in decision making and a score of five was given if the women took decisions independently.

The Decision-Making Index is computed as follows:

$$\text{DMI} = \frac{\text{Decision-making score obtained for woman*}}{\text{Maximum possible score of women}} 100 \quad \text{.........................(1)}$$

The DMI score was grouped as low (0-40), medium (41-70) and high (71-100), based on the range of DMI score. Then, DMI has been treated as the dependant variable and various socio-economic and demographic factors were taken into consideration as independent variables. The study has thus made an attempt to identify the factors that influenced the economic empowerment of women in the carpet industry of Bhadohi by applying multiple linear regression analysis. For this purpose, the following functional form was established.

$$X=f(S,F) \quad \text{...(2)}$$

The specific form of the regression is

$$X = A\, S_i\, F_j\, e \quad \text{..(3)}$$

S_i = is a vector of socio economic variables of women, i = 1........6

Fi = is a vector of freedom of choice variable of women, j = 7

Equation (3) can be rewritten as

$$\text{X= A S1 S2 S3 S4 S5 S6 F7 e} \quad \text{..............................(4)}$$

The specific form of equation (4) is

$$\text{DMI} = \beta_0 + \beta_1\text{WL} + \beta_2\text{WY} + \beta_3\text{NW} + \beta_4\text{OP} + \beta_5\text{HOH} + \beta_6\text{WAGES} + \beta_7\,\text{WRS} + \mu$$

where,

DMI = Decision Making Index(DMI)

WL = Work location

WY = Working years NW = Nature of work

OP = Ownership of property

HoH = Headship of the household

WAGES = Wages of women

WRS =Woman's right to spend

β_0 is the intercept of the model and âiare the parameters of the explanatory variables while μ stands for the stochastic error term to capture all variation in DMI that cannot be explained by the included independent variables in the model.

Participation of women in decision making on different aspects

Participation in decision making on domestic activities

The field survey revealed that women in the study region played an insignificant role in decision making with regard to domestic matters (table-1). Around 42 per cent of women said that they had no right to take decision, even their opinion is not asked for on domestic activities. Around 4.5 per cent reported that they had the final decision in these matters. On the other hand, 22.7 and 23 per cent of women respectively stated that male members asked for opinion only and considered women's advice to some extent. Generally, in matters like gap in child birth, education, and marriage of children. it is the men of the household who made the main decisions.

Table - 1: Participation in decision making by women in domestic activities

Type of Activity	*No partici pation*	*Only opinion asked*	*To some extent*	*To a large extent*	*Final decision*	*Total*
Purchase of food items	0	16	36	26	22	100
Purchase of non-food items	28	50	14	8	0	100
Number of children	60	22	18	0	0	100
Gap in child birth	60	20	20	0	0	100
Education of children	60	16	18	6	0	100
Children's marriage	46	12	32	4	6	100
Total (%)	42.3	22.7	23.0	7.3	4.7	100.0

Source: Calculations based on primary data.

Participation in decision making on money related matters

Participation of women is much less in money related matters. Only 7 per cent of the women respondents said that their advice was listened to in money related matters such as buying and sale of land and animals, expenditure on luxury items, investment, time division between work, leisure and household (table-2). Another 11.5 per cent of the respondents said that they were consulted to some extent, while hardly 1.5 per cent reported that they took independent decisions on these matters. These women belonged to families in which women are old and head of the family or the male member is working outside the district/state.

Table - 2: Participation of women in decision making of women on money related matters

Type of activity	*No participation*	*Only opinion asked*	*To some extent*	*To a large extent*	*Final decision*	*Total*
Control over income	18	52	18	4	8	100
Buying and sale of land and animals	68	20	4	8	0	100
Taking debt for domestic needs	78	10	10	2	0	100
Expenditure on luxury items	74	14	4	8	0	100
Savings	40	44	12	4	0	100
Investment	60	26	6	8	0	100
Time division between work, leisure and household	14	44	26	14	2	100
Total (%)	50.3	30.0	11.4	6.9	1.4	100.0

Source: Calculations based on primary data.

Freedom of women to go outside home

The issue was further explored by asking about the extent of freedom of movement for different purposes. The results are summarised in table-3. Around 24 per cent, of women reported that they had to take permission to attend social functions, purchase something for herself and to go to the hospital, market, and out of the village. However, 32 per cent of women responded that they had to inform the family elders while going out. Around 28 per cent of the respondents stated that they could go out as they wished. Thus, women enjoyed limited autonomy in deciding about their movement outside the home. However, the degree of freedom depended on the age of the woman and her position in the family.

Table - 3: Freedom to go outside the home by purpose of visit

Type of activity	*Have to obey*	*Have to take permission*	*Have to inform only*	*Can go out as they wish*	*Total*
Go to hospital or doctor	0	32	36	32	100
Go to social function	4	10	46	40	100
Purchase something for herself	4	22	40	34	100
Go to market	4	38	26	32	100
Go outside village for work	66	18	12	4	100
Total (%)	15.6	24	32	28.4	100

Source: Authors' calculation based on primary data.

Women decision making index

Women's economic empowerment signifies their power in the household. It means how much say she has in the household matters as well as on matters outside. Some variables were selected and the decision making power has been measured on a five- point scale, where 1 signifies no power to decide and 5 signifies complete power to decide.

Using 24 supporting variables, acomplex index was computed to assess women's participation in economic decision making. The value of EEI ranges from 0 to 100. Women were divided into three levels: high, medium and low. The lowest group ranged from 0-40, the medium group from 41-70 and the highest from 71-100. The economic empowerment was the highest among the group in the range of the 70-100. The EEI included women empowerment variables - both quantitative and qualitative to measure the economic empowerment of women in the carpet industry.

Table-4 reveals the decision making power of women on the basis of the data collected. The study reflects the poor status of women: 58 per cent of women fell in the bracket of low empowerment category, 30 per cent in the medium category and only 12 per cent were in the high empowerment category. Majority of women engaged in the carpet industry had low decision making power which makes them vulnerable in the household.

Table - 4: Distribution of respondents by decision making index

DMI score	*Number of respondents*	*Percentage share in total*
Low (0-40)	29	58
Medium (41-70)	15	30
High (71-100)	6	12
Total	50	100

Factors affecting decision making power of women

There are many factors which affect the decision making power of women such as age, size of the family, type of family, religion and many other social and traditional factors. Women's decision-making power is expected to be higher if they go out to work in manufacturing units instead of working at home. If a woman is skilled and has more experience of working, she is likely to exercise independent decision making. If a woman is aged as ammother, grand-mother, her advice is taken seriously but if she is the head of the household for one reason or other, she is supposed to take all the required decisions independently. Ownership of property also affects women's decision making power and if her wages are high and she has the right to spend her earnings then her decision making power is likely to be high.

Regression analysis confirms these findings (table-5). The DMI is a dependent variable while other variables such as location of work, working years, nature of work, ownership of property, headship of household, woman's right to spend, and wages have been treated as independent variables which determine the DMI. All the independent variables have a positive relationship with the DMI. Location of work, headship of household and women's right to spend are highly significant. The women were much more empowered when they went out to work in the factory and the coefficients of nature of work and ownership of property are also positive but they are not much significant. The wages of a woman had a positive and a very significant impact on her empowerment. As the wages of women increase, the empowerment level also rises. The value of adjusted r-square is 0.856. This indicates that these seven factors are explaining around 85 per cent variation in the decision making index of women working in the carpet industry.

Table - 5: Multiple linear regression between DMI and socio-economic variables

Independent variables	*Coefficients*	*Standard error*	*T-value*	*Significance*
Intercept	-32.192	7.348	-4.381	0.000
location work	7.817	1.995	3.918	0.000
working years	1.881	0.919	2.047	0.047
nature of work	0.730	1.628	0.448	0.656
ownership of property	2.560	2.238	1.144	0.259
headship of household	24.451	3.270	7.478	0.000
Women's right to spend	7.319	1.188	6.161	0.000
Wages	3.140	1.076	2.918	0.006

Note: Dependent Variable = Decision Making Index (DMI).
Adjusted R2 = 0.856.

Conclusion

The study found that the decision making power of women in the carpet industry of Bhadohi was, on the whole, very low. The decision making index shows that only 12 per cent of the women studied of had high decision making, while 58 per cent have low level of decision making, and 30 per cent had medium level of decision making in the household. Wages seemed to enhance the empowerment of women but many factors were in play. Women can be empowered through higher mobility to work and higher wages. Though this study was concerned with economic and mobility factors, it was found that low and insignificant level of education did not play any role in empowering women.

Recommendations

Equity in Payment: Women workers are often underpaid as compared to their male counterparts. Equity in payment is one of the important steps which can help increase the decision making of women workers. Gender bias leads to lower level of confidence among women and therefore lowers the decision making power.

Education Attainment: Education is the biggest and most effective weapon to enhance the welfare of women. These women workers are uneducated and therefore mostly unaware of their rights. They are often misguided, underpaid, etc., due to their lack of knowledge. Education will surely equip them with a better understanding of the situation and better management of their lives. They can claim their rights and this would certainly increase the decision making power of women workers.

Campaign by Government: Even women who were earning had low decision making power. This clearly signifies that the problem lies in the mindset of the society. The government needs to promote welfare and equity of women workers in small scale industries such as carpet industry. The role of government is crucial in empowering women workers and thus raising their level of decision making within the household.

Supporting Mobility and Independence: The decision making power can increase through support by family members and particularly of female members. This support increases mobility, independence and boosts confidence and increases women decision making in households.

8

Micro Entrepreneurial Activities Among Tribal Women in Andhra Pradesh

Krishnaveni Motha

Abstract

Micro enterprises account for major share of employment in developing countries and three quarters of the women make or supplement livelihood through these enterprises, in both rural and urban areas. But it is not always trouble-free for women to take up these activities. They have to overcome various socio-cultural hurdles and limited available resources. The present study aims at finding out the structural attributes of Koya tribal society to take up these activities. The study also evaluates the level of involvement of tribal women in enterprise management and the constraining factors associated with the entrepreneurial activities. A sample of 210 Koya woman entrepreneurs from 6 blocks of Rampachodavaram revenue division of East Godavari district in Andhra Pradesh were selected by using purposive snowball technique. Mixed research methods (both quantitative and qualitative) were applied to collect and analyse the data. Quantitative methods like interview schedule and 10-point enterprise involvement index were used for collection of the socio-economic traits, enterprise details, enterprise involvement and constraints faced by them. Qualitative methods, i.e., focus group discussions, observations and in-depth interviews were applied for analysing the structural attributes of the Koya tribal society. The findings revealed that to earn more through enterprises was the main economic motive of tribal women entering into entrepreneurial activities, limiting their activities to their small geographical areas.

Government interventions and training also motivated the women to take up micro entrepreneurial activities. The study also describes the structural attribute of Koya society where women are treated as economic asset encouraging them into entrepreneurial activities without any socio-cultural hurdles irrespective of their agricultural background. The extent of involvement of women in enterprise management, projected through enterprise involvement index, shows that the time spent by Koya women in entrepreneurial activities was reported to be the highest, while membership in community organisations was found to be the lowest on the 10-point dimensional scale. Stiff competition with non-tribals, lack of access to credit, inadequate knowledge and awareness about marketing strategies, and weak transport system were the constraints in carrying out entrepreneurial activities mentioned by the women.

Introduction

Micro enterprises account mostly for employment in developing countries, and three quarters of the women make or supplement livelihood through these enterprises in rural and urban areas. Over the past decade, micro enterprises have come to be increasingly accepted as a way to improving livelihoods in rural areas especially among women. This trend of transformation in livelihood approaches has also been observed among tribal communities in many parts of India, largely due to loss of collective ownership of lands and other natural resources, introduction of dominant outsiders in their private properties and deforestation, and so on. Numerous factors are contributing to their disadvantageous situation, deepening the poverty among tribals especially women in recent times. Low literacy level excludes them from job opportunities and community management roles. In order to sustain themselves and families, tribal women who were completely unfamiliar to entrepreneurial activities are also starting up micro enterprises, limiting their activities to their small geographical areas, Tribal women are also considering micro entrepreneurial activities as a broader livelihood strategy. It is acknowledged that increasing women's access to entrepreneurial activities is likely to increase overall household income and improve their quality of life.

But it is not always trouble-free for women to take up such activities. They have to overcome various socio-cultural hurdles and share the limited available resources in rural and tribal areas. The eco system of woman entrepreneurship is not always healthy due to various socio-cultural and gender attributes prevailing in the societies of which they are a part. These attributes can influence both positively and negatively the emergence of entrepreneurship in the tribal areas. Despite many anticipated benefits of participation of tribal women in micro entrepreneurial activities, the number of tribal women engaged in them in India is very small.

The paper begins with reviewing the literature on tribal entrepreneurs in general and, more specifically, tribal woman entrepreneurs operating in various parts of India. Section-2 of the paper highlights the methodology followed to conduct the study among the Koya tribal women in the study area, followed in section-3 by findings and discussion. The findings reveals that all woman entrepreneurs in the study area were not enganged in entrepreneurial activities due to economic necessity, but to earn more through enterprises and improve their quality of life. The findings strongly demonstrate that the healthy eco system of Koyas was more of a social asset to women rather than a source of hindrance or constraint to starting micro enterprises for their livelihood which is in was contrast to the findings of studies conducted in the past.

Review of research

This section reviews the research done so far on tribal entrepreneurship in India, leading to the present study. During 1970s and 80s, studies conducted on entrepreneurial activities among the tribals in India exemplify the attributes and traits of tribal entrepreneurial activities, change in the occupational structure of the tribals, motivational factors and reasons for entrepreneurship endeavour in tribal and urban areas in India. Some of the prominent studies conducted in the past are discussed below.

Sachidanand (1968) revealed that tribals show entrepreneurship traits by opening grocery, tea and cycle repair shops in the tribal areas of Bihar. He observed that a new class of money-lenders had emerged out of the tribals themselves, who were exploiters similar to non-tribal money-lenders. According to him, the traditional tribal economy has been affected by monetisation. The community was moving in the direction of integration into wider social, economic and political system of the nation. Bogaert (1972), who studied tribal entrepreneurs of Ranchi, observed that unlike the non-tribal entrepreneurs, the tribals were motivated by the spirit of profit-making and the desire to strengthen social relations with their kinsmen by assisting them in apparently disinterested tasks. In another study in the same region, Bogaert et al. (1972) found that tribal entrepreneurs in Ranchi were engaged in diverse avenues of self-employment activities. He concluded that these first generation entrepreneurs had a weak financial basis as they depended mainly on their own limited funds. Tribals were lacking in business skills/tactics, and also there was absence of awareness of opportunities. Regarding the emergence of entrepreneurial activities in tribal societies, Tridevi (1991) stated that entrepreneurial activities had come to the tribals more or less as a movement which had introduced some basic structural changes in the Bhil tribal society of Rajasthan, India. Srinivas (1995) informed that under self-employment schemes, Koya tribal people of Warangal district of Andhra Pradesh had started small businesses in essential commodities, rice milling and hotels in villages, which is contributing to the emergence of new tribal entrepreneurship. The emergence of large number of indigenous educated and first generation tribal entrepreneurs is an indication of the emergence of an entrepreneurial class within the Khashi tribal society in East Khashi hill district of Meghalaya (Srivastav and Syngkon 2007).

In order to contribute to the development of entrepreneurship in tribal areas, this section also reviewed some specific studies which focused on the development of entrepreneurship among tribals. Encouraging entrepreneurship among tribal people has been advocated as the most promising avenue for economic development among tribal communities. Singh (1974) suggested that, while developing entrepreneurship among tribals requires different treatment in the developed and under-developed areas because the industrial culture and socio-economic conditions for these two types of areas were entirely different. He observed that the entrepreneur in a backward area often depends on imitation than on innovation. In his study of entrepreneurship in a backward region, Parmeshwaram (1975) observed that the principle of social marginality was more applicable than the principle of achievement motivation in the backward areas.

While developing a model for entrepreneurship in primitive society by way of a case study of tribal entrepreneurs in Gujarat, Moulik (1975) reveals how the contrasting entrepreneurial types with primitive background come into being in tribal societies. While talking about entrepreneurship development in tribal societies, Singh (1976) mentioned the need to locate ways of dealing with the socio-cultural factors of the tribal people in the Chotanagpur belt of Bihar in accepting an innovation like electricity.

Choudary (1981) studied the entrepreneurial activities in the north-eastern region of India in order to find out their identity in terms of social, local, occupational and product-wise variations. Inter-state variations in tribal entrepreneurship were observed: in Manipur, Mizoram and Meghalaya the tribal entrepreneurial activities were more, whereas states like Assam, Tripura and Nagaland supplied less number of entrepreneurs in proportion to population. For developing entrepreneurial activities among tribals, holistic approach is needed wherein all the cultural and social aspects of the client community should be studied thoroughly (Sethy 1981). The nature and extent of entrepreneurship among tribal societies were believed to account for their differential rates of development Khanka and Bisht (1987).

Arora and Bhandari (1999) highlighted the socio-economic conditions of tribals in Andhra Pradesh, who were being exploited by traders with high rate of interest on money borrowed and lower prices for minor forest produce sold by them. The study recommended that the tribals engaged in minor forest produce collection should be encouraged to establish their own cooperative societies and the tribals having entrepreneurial qualities may be given training in processing the minor forest produce and managing the cooperative societies.

Dandhi and Intodia (2001) observed that the problem of unemployment cannot be solved unless the educated rural and tribal youth were trained and involved in entrepreneurship oriented courses, in their study in the districts of Dungarpur, Banswara, Udaipur and

Chittorgarh in Rajasthan. Same rationale was exposed by Saxena, Kukreti and Gihar (2004) who suggested that, to overcome the low participation rates in entrepreneurial activities among tribal youth in Rajasthan, entrepreneurship curriculum should be introduced at school/ college level for a favourable change in their attitude towards entrepreneurship. Entrepreneurial activities can bridge the gap between rural and urban areas. While promoting entrepreneurship, issues like proper skill development, market support, hand holding support and strengthening the extension services can build up the competencies and efficacy of the tribal people (Kumar 2012).

While studying entrepreneurial behaviour among the tribals, it was found that tribal fish farmer entrepreneurs of Tripura possessed medium level of innovativeness, motivation, risk taking ability and leadership qualities. Tailor-made entrepreneurship development programmes based on the attributes can boost entrepreneurial interest in aqua culture sector of the state (Pandey and De 2015).

Barriers to tribal entrepreneurship

Entrepreneurship development in tribal communities is a basically complex process of change. Studies conducted on tribal entrepreneurship in India reveal that tribal entrepreneurs face considerable handicaps arising from their own culture and value system like weak financial base, low risk taking due to pre-capitalistic attitude towards money, absence of technical and business skills, lack of awareness of opportunities, low capacity to cooperate effectively with one another on business terms, absence of training facilities and information, and lack of effective communication between the government and the people. Bogaert (1975) conducted a pilot study on urban entrepreneurship amongst tribals living in Ranchi and Khunti, a sub-divisional town of the Ranchi district. He suggested that handicaps faced by tribals were not insurmountable, and flow of adequate financial assistance and provision for training facilities should help to overcome them.

Neog (1984) in his paper mentioned that tribal society is characterised by limited literacy and provision of official job reservation which lessen the attraction for private industrialisation.

Socio-political reasons may not allow launching of industrialisation through a class of 'borrowed entrepreneurs'. Socio-psychological attitude towards industrial development in some tribals was not very helpful. That the problems faced by the tribal entrepreneurs were not similar and identical, but were individual in nature was mentioned by Mali (1989) while studying the development of tribal entrepreneurship in the north-eastern region of India.

Parthasarathi (2000) conducted comparative study on economic status of tribal and non-tribal entrepreneurs of Paderu mandal of Andhra Pradesh. The results highlighted that majority of entrepreneurs switched over to business due to inadequacy of income in their former occupations. The entrepreneurs were facing many problems such as injustice from money-lenders, high rate of interest, local competition, transport bottlenecks and lack of financial assistance from banks.

Lack of assets, high rate of interest, problem of re-investment, lack of skills, awareness, location factor, communication problem and marketing were identified as the major problems faced by tribal woman entrepreneurs in the tribal sub-plan region of Udaipur, Dungarpur and Banswara of Rajasthan (Dashora and Sharma 2003).

According to the survey conducted in Mandar block of Ranchi district, the reasons for the prevailing poor entrepreneurial practices among tribals in these regions were due to the social attitude, inadequate infrastructure, lack of proper training and development, and poor delivery mechanism of the services (Kumar 2012).

An exploratory study was conducted in Mayurbhanj district of Orissa to know the tribal entrepreneurs' access to credit with a view to assessing their knowledge and practice of lending by formal and informal financial institutions by Mohapatra, Behera and Sahu (2012). It illustrated that credit facilities were not adequate for the tribal entrepreneurs in the district, interest rates varied in relation to types of loan by financial institutions, and informal financial institutions charged higher rate of interest than formal ones.

Biswal (2013) stated that most of the tribals were first generation entrepreneurs who were facing both external and internal problems like infrastructure, transportation, poor financial assistance and credit facilities, inadequate power supply, lack of managerial skills and technical knowledge, and lack of awareness of government schemes in the state of Meghalaya.

Tribal women and entrepreneurial activities

Overall, the literature on tribal women entrepreneurship is scarce and meagre in the Indian context. In spite of growing importance of entrepreneurship development for reducing the economic disparity among urban and rural areas, and micro enterprises accepted as a means of improving livelihoods in rural and tribal areas especially among women, little is known about Indian tribal women entrepreneurship.

Neog (1984) stated that it is wrong to accept that tribal societies entirely lacked entrepreneurship. Female tribal entrepreneurs had greater likelihood of success if they were recruited from higher age groups with lower prospect of getting married, and widows, separated wives or spinsters. Jagirdar (1986) stated that women's entrepreneurship and participation in economic productivity were positive indicators which directly helped the developmental process in Minyong tribal society of north- eastern region of India.

Dashora and Sharma (2003) in their study of tribal women entrepreneurs found that tribal women have come a long way, breaking the shackles of tribal community and are engaged themselves in occupations other than agriculture. More tribal women are inclined towards entrepreneurship and acquired greater business aptitude.

Reporting the findings of research project on multi-factorial nature of women's role in economic development in Meghalaya, Kurbah (2013) stated that the findings strongly demonstrated no gender bias, and matrilineal tending did not dampen the role of women in entrepreneurship in Khasi tribal society. In fact, Khasi tribal culture strongly influences the promoting of entrepreneurial traits among women who have been able to build an economic basis.

Thaker and Ahlwat (2012) in their study identified that majority of tribal women in the Banaskantha district of Gujarat were having low socio-economic profile, communications and medium level of entrepreneurial attributes. Tribal women were mostly interested in activities like animal husbandry and dairy based enterprises, followed by food based and agro based, which were already taken up as a source of livelihood and wanted to convert the same into potential enterprises.

Lack of access to capital has been a major obstacle to tribal entrepreneurship in India. Rather than taking a narrow, purely financial, view of capital the studies also explore a wider range of constraints faced by tribal entrepreneurs in various parts of India. Tribal dairy entrepreneurs in the Mayurbhanj district of Orissa were facing constraints of high cost of concentrate, lack of availability of veterinary literature, non-remunerative price for milk, poor irrigation facilities for growing fodder crops for livestock animals (Mohapatra, Behera, and Sahu, 2012).

While studying the various entrepreneurial activities among women of Sonowal Kachari tribal society of Dibrugarh district in Assam, the author stated that women in recent times have taken up entrepreneurial activities for improving their economic status. But it has been observed that, like other community women, the rate of growth of women entrepreneurship is not adequate due to some basic problems arising in relation to entrepreneurial development in these societies. The main problems faced by the women entrepreneurs were lack of education, lack of finance, lack of training and marketing facilities (Hazarira 2013), which needs to be addressed.

Regarding the problems faced by tribal woman entrepreneurs engaged in cottage industries of Dhag district of Gujarat, Bhatt (2015) stated that competition with branded products, absence of the advertisement cost and technological knowledge, poor infrastructure facilities, etc., were the main problems. By providing support to these entrepreneurs by government and other institutions, income of the entrepreneurs can be increased and economic disparity between rural and urban sectors can be reduced.

Researching on tribal woman entrepreneurs in bamboo based handicraft sector in Tripura, Deb (2015) illustrated that basically women have taken up entrepreneurial activities due to poverty. These women have received loans from various government and non-development organisations for taking up the activities which helped them to improve their economic status. Women also mentioned about the barriers faced by them due to dearth of awareness about technologies, scarcity of raw materials and transportation problems for smooth running of enterprises. Lalhunthara (2015) mentioned that the women came out as less entrepreneurial than men while conducting a study in Mizoram. Hence government should create programmes especially for development of women entrepreneurship and women cells.

Purpose of the study

A wide stream of research has explored the emergence of entrepreneurial activities among tribals in India. Research studies in the past attempted to identify the nature and type of entrepreneurship among the tribals, traits and problems of tribal entrepreneurs nationwide. With a few exceptions much of the literature reports about tribal entrepreneurial activities among men and women mostly in the northern and north-eastern parts of India. Until now, in consequence, much work on tribal entrepreneurs has not been done in the southern part of India. The present study aims at finding out the micro entrepreneurial activities among Koya tribal women in a southern state of India: Andhra Pradesh. Koyas are the second largest tribal population in Andhra Pradesh and have unique socio-cultural background. They mainly inhabit the hilly areas of the West Godavari, East Godavari, Khammam and Warangal districts of Andhra Pradesh.

The study tries to explore in depth the reasons for women venturing into entrepreneurial activities and what structural attributes of Koya tribal society were associated with these activities. The study also tries to evaluate the level of involvement of tribal women in enterprise management and the constraining factors associated with entrepreneurial activities.

Research method

The present study focuses on the entrepreneurial activities of Koya tribal women of Rampachodavaram revenue division in the East Godavari district of Andhra Pradesh, India. Observing and probing the entrepreneurs in tribal areas was a difficult and complex process. The working definition of the tribal woman entrepreneurs used in the study was as follows:"A tribal woman entrepreneur is one who organises, manages the enterprise by herself or with the help of family members, and produces and markets the products within the tribal or nearby areas".

The selection of the sample was a tedious process as none of the enterprises run by the Koya woman entrepreneurs were registered and no records or other obvious sources were available for locating tribal woman entrepreneurs in the study area. Majority of the entrepreneurs had taken up entrepreneurial activities on their own initiative without approaching any agencies, except the members of SHGs who had taken loans from their groups.

The sample was selected by using purposive snowball technique as it was difficult for the researcher to access the tribal entrepreneurs due to geographical conditions of the sample area. The researcher requested the woman entrepreneurs first identified to nominate through their social networks other tribal woman entrepreneurs who fitted the profile and could potentially contribute to a specific study. Thus a sample of 210 tribal entrepreneurs from 6 blocks of Rampachodavaram revenue division of East Godavari district of Andhra Pradesh were approached through local people. So the number of entrepreneurs studied from each block varies from the other, as they were not equally distributed.

In the present study mixed research methods (both quantitative and qualitative) were applied to analyse the data, mainly due to the fact that such methods can yield better results as the limitations of one method are balanced by the other through its strengths. As it is not always possible for structured schedules to get the information from the tribal/indigenous people due to various socio-cultural factors, in such situation qualitative data helped to understand these factors and supported collection of data for the study. Quantitative methods are useful in measuring the extent and pattern of outcomes of the study through various sources like survey and statistical records. With this view, quantitative methods like interview schedule and 10-point enterprise involvement index were used for collection of the Koya women's socio- economic traits, enterprise details and enterprise involvement. Qualitative methods like observations, focus group discussions, and case study methods were applied for analysing the structural attributes of the Koya tribe and to bring about in-depth perceptual facts about the traits which helped the Koya women to venture into entrepreneurial activities. Interactions with officials of various organisations like Integrated Tribal Development Agency (ITDA), and Girijan Cooperative Corporation (GCC) also helped to determine the government role in helping the Koya woman entrepreneurs

Findings of the study

The research objectives that guided this study were:

1. To explore the reasons for women to venture into entrepreneurial activities and structural attributes of Koya tribal society that contributed to taking up these activities
2. To evaluate the level of involvement of tribal women in enterprise management and constraining factors associated with entrepreneurial activities.

Before highlighting the findings, a glimpse of the background of Koya women is presented to enable understanding of the relationship between Koya society and entrepreneurial activities taken up by the women in the study area.

Background of Koya woman entrepreneurs

This section explores the social traits of the Koya woman entrepreneurs who belonged to various age groups, with the youngest falling in the group of below 25 years and the oldest above 50 years. Majority of woman entrepreneurs belonged to the middle age group (35-50 years). As far as family type is concerned, majority belonged to nucleus type of families. It is customary among the Koyas for the son to separate from parents and establish a new home, which may be the reason for most of the women having average family size of 3 to 5 members. More than 90 per cent of the women had children to take care of as most of them were in the middle age group. This indicates that majority of Koya women in the study area had to carry out their entrepreneurial activities along with household work and childcare which also explains the reasons for operating their businesses from their homes.

The educational levels of Koya women ranged from those who had never been to school to those who studied up to high school. However, more than half of the women entrepreneurs were illiterate. Very few of them had the opportunity to study up to high school level. None of the women running forest based enterprises had studied up to high school level. It can be noted that low levels of education have not hindered the Koya women from venturing into business and establishing their own enterprises.

The economic structure of Koya tribal society mainly depends on land, forest and forest resources. Among the 210 Koya women interviewed, 139 women were practising agriculture for the past so many years, while rest of them were landless labourers, wage earners, etc. Almost all the entrepreneurs were small and marginal farmers having 1 to 5 acres of land. Basically Koyas practised podu/shifting cultivation; slowly with interventions by the Government, they have taken up settled agriculture. Most of their household economy also depends on minor forest produce which play an important role in the viability and survival of tribal households in Andhra Pradesh. Due to subsistence economy, most of the tribal households were also found to be involved in subsidiary occupations to earn livelihoods during non- agricultural seasons.

Type of enterprises

Entrepreneurial activities in the tribal areas are quite different from their counterparts due to hostile environment. Their enterprises are very much related to forest or geographical background and their businesses often vary with agricultural seasons. Many of the micro enterprises are not autonomous economic enterprises, but are part of large family or household enterprises. The cash associated with one's enterprise frequently mingles with that of other household activities. This is particularly true in case of enterprises owned and operated by women (Mohiuddin 2002).

In the present context, tribal women were operating 5 different types of enterprises with majority of the first generation entrepreneurs involved in trade and service sector such as petty shops, hotels and kirana shops. The second generation entrepreneurs, who preferred the activities similar to their parent occupation, were mostly engaged in forest based enterprises. These enterprises were usually based on traditional/indigenous skills of the tribal folk. The period of involvement in entrepreneurial activities by the Koya women varied from less than 5 years to more than 25 years, with average period of 4.97 years, indicating that the woman entrepreneurs were still in the process of establishment.

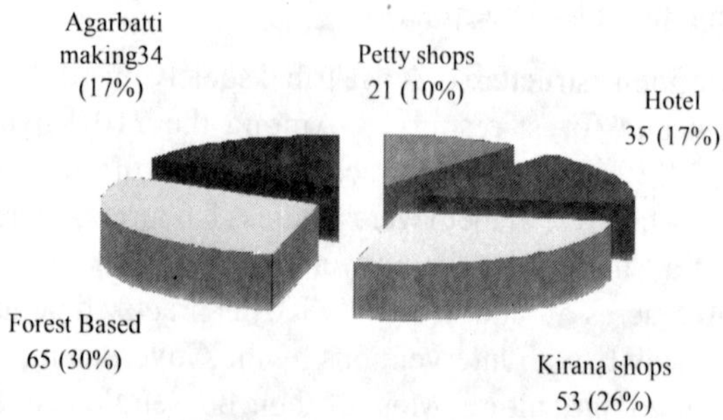

Fig. 1: Type of enterprises run by tribal women

Reasons of tribal women entrepreneurship

In brief, concerning the first research objective, it was found that the main reason behind entrepreneurship among tribal women was to earn more from enterprises along with their traditional occupations. The objective of the study further highlighted that socio-cultural attributes of Koya tribal society were more of constructive nature than of hindrance to entrepreneurial activities.

An important finding of the study was, tribal women mainly entered the enterprises to earn more and improve the quality of life, even though in some cases women were forced to take up entrepreneurial activities due to lack of employment opportunities in farm sector and less income from daily wages. Forest based entrepreneurs consistently reported that their ventures were motivated by economic and social dimensions of family and they were home based enterprises associated with land and forest, operating away from their parents. Entrepreneurs were also motivated by external factors like encouragement by the stakeholders of government schemes to start up the enterprise, especially in case of agarbatti making, after receiving the training.

A series of interviews with 210 tribal women bought into focus the socio-cultural attributes of Koya tribal society. The findings did not resonate well with other relevant published studies on women entrepreneurship, which revealed that women in both rural and urban areas faced socio-cultural discrimination in taking up micro entrepreneurial activities. The findings from in-depth interviews and case studies strongly demonstrated that there were no socio-cultural restrictions and gender bias in respect of Koya women for entering into entrepreneurial activities. One important factor noticed in the present context was that, for tribal woman entrepreneurs family gave considerable support without any socio-cultural restrictions. In this respect, the family set-up was considered more a social asset for business, rather than as a hindrance or constraint. It was held that by virtue of a conducive social system among the tribals especially in Koya society, where woman is treated as economic asset of the family, women have been contributing substantially towards their own family incomes and improving the standard of living of their families on the one hand and also enriching tribal wealth on the other, through entrepreneurial activities. These structural attributes are promoting enduring entrepreneurial traits among tribal women who were earlier only confined to land and forest related activities.

Tribal women in micro enterprise management

Bench-marking women's participation in firm ownership, management, and work-force is important to achieving gender equality promotion and empowerment of women (World Bank survey). Numerous studies carried out on effective participation of women in management reveal that women's participation in management removes socio-institutional barriers and enhances the capabilities to engage, influence and beheld accountable to the functions of their enterprises. Despite their instrumental role in running business, women continue to be excluded from enterprise management in many household enterprises. The central focus of the present study was to evaluate the level of involvement by Koya women in the management of their enterprises. To measure involvement, an enterprise involvement index (R.K. Padai scale) on 10 dimensions namely motivation, setting up the enterprise, management of the enterprise, decision making, time spent on enterprise, level of satisfaction, pride on being an entrepreneur, member in associations,training in skill development, and future plans was adopted. For each of these 10 dimension responses from the Koya women were quantified on a scale of 1 to 5 and averages were computed for each facet and rankings given to identify the crucial dimensions that are relatively strong in the enterprise involvement index.

Motivation

One of the vital facets of the study was to authenticate the factors that motivated the Koya women to start the enterprises. Among the five factors of motivation, it was self- motivation of the Koya women which forced them to start and earn more through establishing enterprises. Family was the second major source of motivation and helped them to carry out entrepreneurial activities smoothly without any role conflicts. Entrepreneurs were also motivated by the stakeholders in case of agarbatti making enterprises.

Setting up of the enterprise

With regard to setting up the enterprise, most of the Koya women stated that they themselves tried to set up the enterprise on their own without involving others, while others stated that the help of their family had been the major facilitating factor in setting up the enterprises. The families had provided them the financial assets, physical and human assets for setting up the enterprise to some, while for others relatives and friends had lent a helping hand.

Management of the enterprise

Tribal women lack the opportunity rather than the capacity. It has been recognised through the study that self-development and capacity building can be strengthened by entrusting tribal women with direct management of the enterprise. Production, procurement of raw materials and mobilising the credit were the functions handled independently by 34.28 per cent of the entrepreneurs, whereas another 33.80 per cent were taking help of the family members. This analysis clearly indicates that woman entrepreneurs are more or less self-reliant in managing their business.

Decision making

In general, decision-making is a complex process and a challenging task, which may involve a series of stages and people. Decision making in business is a very sensitive issue as it involves key decision areas such as money/income, ownership and control. In the present study, woman entrepreneurs themselves were major decision makers in case of 34.28 per cent of enterprises, whereas 35.71 per cent entrepreneurs had consulted their family members in taking major decisions concerning their enterprise activities. However, some decisions they make may be influenced by their husbands as most of the enterprises owned by the women were home based. Around 24.28 per cent of the woman entrepreneurs claimed that they made decisions jointly with other entrepreneurs, as their enterprises were joint ventures. Only in very few cases women were passive in decision making matters, even though they were investing considerable time in the enterprise and yet not identifying themselves as enterprise owners. This may be one hindering factor that made them not to grow professionally and demonstrate entrepreneurial attitudes.

Time spent on enterprise

A number of studies enlightened that time is a precious resource for woman entrepreneurs especially those who ran the business along with their families. Women in all types of enterprises spend long hours in entrepreneurial activities along with their household activities. They stated that they were able to spare long hours for entrepreneurial activities because of having the enterprises next to nearby their homes. Gender and Rural Employment Policy Brief # 3, 2010 stated that this is one of the advantages of micro enterprises which offered flexible hours, location in or near women's home, ease of entry and links with local markets.

Level of satisfaction

Work satisfaction is essential in performing any activity. More than half of the women entrepreneurs (51.42 per cent) expressed moderate satisfaction. Nearly 20 per cent of woman entrepreneurs expressed high satisfaction, and wished to expand and diversify their units for earning more. Most of these entrepreneurs mentioned that the returns from their enterprises were satisfactory. The success of these enterprises also confers on the Koya woman entrepreneur a great sense of pride and personal satisfaction and gives them a feeling of worth and status in their families and the Koya society.

Membership in community organisations

Membership in business associations can be important not only for increasing the chances of accessing support services, but also for the purpose of networking and information/experience sharing amongst the members. Effective representation in community based or civil society organisations will provide an opportunity to state their priorities, needs, interests and expectations to be taken into consideration. Such situations virtually lead to accessibility to resources and opportunities for them. The study shows that significant number of women belonged to village level organisations formed by the SHGs. Moreover, the creation of SHGs has provided these women with a structure for mutual support which proved particularly effective in empowering women by striving collectively for social change as well as being a powerful tool in promoting the concept of self-reliance. In a nutshell, it has clearly benefited the Koya women in many ways, not only by facilitating micro credit but also mobility, social visibility, dignity and self-esteem.

Table - 1: Tribal women in micro enterprise management

Dimensions		*Frequency*	*Mean score*	*Rank*
Motivation	Own	74(35.23)	**3.32**	**3**
	Own +Others	3(1.42)		
	Own + Friends/other entrepreneurs	54(25.71)		
	Own+ Family	75(35.71)		
	Purely suggested by others	4(1.90)		
Setting up of the enterprise	Own	71(33.80)	**3.29**	**5**
	Own+ Others	6(2.85)		
	Own+ Help Received	54(25.71)		
	Own+ family	71(33.80)		
	Done by others	8(3.80)		
Management of the enterprise	Own	72(34.28)	**3.31**	**4**
	Own+ Others	8(2.85)		
	Own+ Help Received	51(24.28)		
	Own+ family	71(33.80)		
	Done by others	8(3.80)		
Decision making	Entrepreneur Herself	72(34.28)	**3.32**	**3**
	Entrepreneur+ others	8(2.85)		
	Entrepreneurs+ others/Friends	51(24.28)		
	Entrepreneur+ family	75(35.71)		
	Mostly taken by others	4(3.80)		
Time spent	Above 10 hours	87(41.42)	**3.72**	**1**
	8-9 hours	41(19.52)		
	6-8 hours	21(10.00)		
	4-6 hours	60(28.57)		
	2-3 hours	1(0.47)		
Satisfaction level	Highest satisfaction	19(9.04)	**2.92**	**7**
	High Satisfaction	17(8.09)		
	Moderate Satisfaction	108(51.42)		
	Slight Satisfaction	61(29.0)		
	No Change	5(2.38)		
Training	Training Obtained	59(28.09)	**3.02**	**6**
	Need for Training	19(9.04)		
	No need for training	132(62.85)		
Pride being entrepreneur	Highest Score	19(9.04)	**2.92**	**7**
	High score	17(8.09)		
	Moderate Score	108(51.42)		
	Low Score	61(29.04)		
	Lowest Score	5(2.38)		
Membership	Holding position in business associations	-	**2.16**	**8**
	Members in business organizations			
	Holding position in V.L.Os*	33(15.71)		
	Member in SHGs**	106(50.47)		
	Not a member	71(33.89)		
Future plans	Definite Plans & working out	59(28.05)	**3.55**	**2**
	Definite Plans	65(30.92)		
	Some Plans, some ideas	24(11.44)		
	Vague ideas	57(27.1)		
	No plans	5(2.38)		

*Village level organisations **Self-help groups

Training received in skill development

Woman entrepreneurs of agarbatti enterprises had received skill development training for their enterprises and orientation training conducted by the forest department and District Rural Development Agency for members of SHGs. Only a small number of women entrepreneurs expressed the need for training. The study opined that tribal women's access to information can be increased through the various training programmes which will eventually be a motivator for adopting entrepreneurial activities in more sustainable manner for the improvement of quality of life for their families and communities.

Future expansion plans

The study also found that women were committed to their business and had plans for expansion of their business in near future. Majority of the women intended to make new investments. Tribal women expressed the need for access to information, services and micro credit for expansion which were seldom reachable to these enterprises.

Barriers/constraints to entrepreneurial activities

A number of the perceived barriers to entrepreneurial activities were embedded in the tribal system itself. The tribal women running the enterprises mentioned a number of barriers that were interwoven in the fabric of their life style and impeded the growth of enterprises in their own eco system.

Limited access to financial capital

Among the barriers, inadequate finance for re-investment was found to be severe. Main part of finance for starting the enterprises came from personal savings and loans from kinsfolk to most of them which was proving to be continuous barrier when they were trying to mobilise capital for re-investment in the unit and also for expanding their enterprises. Another strong reason was not having access to information about financial sources avavilable, except for some tribal women who were managing to get finance from community based organisations called Self-Help Groups due to their membership, and from forest department. Obtaining capital within the tribal areas is virtually impossible due to absence of formal financial institutions. These entrepreneurs reported inability to secure loans from banks in their needy hour as the formalities involved in obtaining loans were complex and cumbersome. One more limitation was the collateral required by banks which was not possible for these poor women which ultimately forces them to knock the doors of middlemen. Most of the tribal women approach middlemen who charge exorbitant rates of interest on the credit offered to them. Illiteracy limits the tribal woman entrepreneurs from taking advantage of formal sources which in turn affect the pace of their business.

While the findings showed that principal barrier to enterprises was lack of access to credit, the tribal women also stated other prominent barriers which were embedded in their eco system and were inter-related: remoteness , lack of transport facilities and market access, low return, risk bearing capacity, competition and social networks, time constraint, mobility, etc.

Remoteness and lack of transport facilities

One of the main barriers affecting tribal woman enterprises is their remoteness. This problem appeared to be very severe among the entrepreneurs who were especially involved in trading and service sectors, i.e., hotels, petty shops and kirana shops. Due to remoteness, transport costs are higher and local demand is low. Commodities needed for enterprises have to be obtained from urban areas for which travelling can be problematic as they have to walk or travel longer distances due to lack of proper transport facilities. This was adversely affecting the business continuity and impeded the vertical growth of enterprises in the tribal areas.

Lack of market access and low return

Low returns were found to be a severe problem for the entrepreneurs in production, i.e., forest based and agarbatti making enterprises. Lack of market access precludes them from realising tangible benefits from these enterprises. Many women also lack sufficient technological knowledge which limits their access to markets. In all the enterprises, production was carried out either manually or partially with hand tools. The quality of their products was also poor in many cases, compelling them to sell at very low prices, despite considerable time involved in production. Entrepreneurs of forest based enterprises were selling the products to middlemen who were procuring products at low prices, collecting them at the entrepreneurs' doorsteps, so that they could to avoid travelling to market places.

Competition and social networks

Koya women running in enterprises experience conflict in competing aspects of non-tribals. Non-tribals who were outsiders in the tribal eco system were very much dominant and established themselves as entrepreneurs over a period of time, competing with the tribals. Technologically high and well established enterprises of non-tribals are impeding the growth of tribal enterprises in their own topography.

Another barrier encountered by these women was from their own tribal and other tribal groups. Social network among tribes is a rich source of support and also helped the women in establishing their enterprises in the initial stages, but sometimes these networks also acted as a limitation. These social networks even result in draining the resources as tribal women are expected to share their resources through barter system which prevails in Koya economic system. The entrepreneur needs to make profit to succeed in business, but clan groups except support and favours which sometimes overwhelm their new enterprises. This barrier was specifically experienced by the women in trade and service sector.

Risk bearing capacity and lack of business skills

During the interviews, many women expressed that they lacked abilities, skills and expertise in running the business. Majority of the enterprises were developed by first generation entrepreneurs who often lacked business skills. This makes them unwilling to take risk and expand their enterprises. The entrepreneurs had limited knowledge about the programmes and schemes for women entrepreneurship promoted by the government, to take advantage of resources.

Time constraint and mobility problem

One of the most critical constraints identified by tribal woman entrepreneurs throughout the enterprise cycle was lack of time for business. Around 50 per cent of entrepreneurs mentioned that the time constraint was very severe. It was clear from the data that majority of the women in the study area had household responsibilities to fulfill in addition to developing their businesses. Around 30 per cent of the entrepreneurs were not facing this problem as they had the support of their families and the opportunity to have the enterprise as an extension to their homes.

Mobility is the greatest gender specific problem faced by these women in their entire enterprise cycle. Due to socio-cultural restrictions on mobility, many women faced heavy constraints while setting up and running their enterprises. Women are as such free to move and participate in economic activities in many tribal communities. But some women mentioned that due to domestic chores they were unable to mobilise to market places frequently, but not due to socio-cultural restrictions on women's mobility in the tribal society.

Thus the major constraints faced by tribal woman entrepreneurs were related to isolation from market mechanisms transport bottlenecks and unfavourable economic context in which they operate, rather than to gender based factors. Nearly all the tribal women interviewed had severe time constraint because of juggling between business, household and community duties.

Conclusion

Trends of transformation in approaches to livelihood in Koya community were seen in the emergence of entrepreneurial activities among them. Koya women generally involved in agriculture and farm activities were also considering micro enterprise activities as an appropriate or viable livelihood option for improving their quality of life. Interventions by the Government through SHGs in tribal areas helped the women to venture into entrepreneurial line. Majority of the enterprises owned by tribal women were marginal from economic point of view. In the present context tribal enterprises and entrepreneurship continue to make positive contribution to holistic development of tribal peoples and their societies, but challenges like access to credit need to be addressed. Time spent on enterprise activities and future expansion plans for their enterprises clearly show how serious Koya women are about their enterprises. These women need to be nurtured and sensitised about the government programme and given access to information about financial and hand holding services that stimulate growth of their enterprises. Thus entrepreneurship will positively impact enhancing women's access to independent income, their control over the management of household assets and budget. Economic gains are being slowly created by Koya women in their communities and further progress presents a tremendous growth opportunity to the tribal society.

The position of indigenous women in their societies and their contributions to household economy can be better understood by studying the entrepreneurial activities in depth. Policy makers and implementers should encourage entrepreneurship among tribal/ indigenous communities in their own local communities, its deep-seated role in economic growth and development. Lack of research and evaluation hampers the effectiveness of policy efforts to promote entrepreneurship in tribal societies. Extensive research is needed for framing suitable policies and programmes as not much field information is available on tribal entrepreneurship.

9

Woman Entrepreneurs and Financial Literacy: A Study in Selected Districts of Western Odisha

Bhabani Shankar Dash
Bhagaban Das

Abstract

The level of financial literacy among the Indian women has not been well documented. Hence, the need arises to understand in detail the issue of financial literacy among women in India. This paper is an attempt in this direction. Financial literacy has been identified as one of the key competencies required for establishing, managing and thriving of the enterprise. However, the exact effect they have on the financial performance of enterprise has not been fully established by the available literature, therefore the need for further research in this area. This study seeks to establish the influence of financial literacy on the financial performance of women entrepreneurs in selected districts of western Odisha. A descriptive survey design was adopted for conducting the study. A sample of 57 woman entrepreneurs was selected out of the total population, using stratified sampling methods. The data collected was analysed using SPSS and the significance of the results tested using inferential statistics. The results of the multiple regressions revealed that there is a significant strong positive relationship between financial literacy and financial performance of woman entrepreneurs. The study recommends that awareness be created among woman entrepreneurs about the importance of being financially literate by encouraging them to participate in financial literacy training programmes.

Keywords: *Financial planning, literacy, entrepreneurs, encourage, programme, factors*

Introduction

Economic growth and development of the country is determined by human, physical and financial resources. An economy can move on to higher levels of growth either by acquiring a larger quantum of the factors of production or through technical progress. The objective of any planned development is to develop human resources to their brimming utilisation. Therefore, industrialisation is one of the ways of bringing about socio-economic development in any country (Schollhammer & Kwiloff 1933).

The economic development of a nation is sparked largely by its enterprising spirit. The characteristic of enterprising emerges from the inter-play of behaviour and activity of a special segment of the population known as entrepreneurs. India's economy is today poised for flourishing entrepreneurial activity. It is also known that healthy business environment is an essential requirement of entrepreneurial growth. Since a high quality entrepreneurial skill tends to attain industrial growth, talent must come from within the environment for rapid and sustained growth of the economy. A country may be rich in material resources and capital. But if entrepreneurship is lacking, the utilisation of resources would not be as expected. Entrepreneurs are a part of industrial society and as such, they should be considered an asset. The entrepreneur is responsible for not only earning their own livelihood but also for creating avenues of employment for others and contributing to the gross national product (Schollhammer & Kwiloff 1933).

Financial literacy has attracted increasing attention in both the developed and developing countries due to its role in financial decision making. For example, in January 2008, the United States government had set up President's Advisory Council on Financial Literacy, tasked to improve financial education at all levels of the economy. Developing economies too have not been left behind; countries like Indonesia and Ghana have set up programmes that are aimed at increasing financial literacy. Financial literacy encompasses the knowledge and skill required by an individual to function effectively in the monetary economy and make informed judgments in respect of their own and their family circumstances. The need for financial literacy among entrepreneurs and business owners has henceforth become an issue of interest in both the developed and the developing economies (Lacity & Jansen 1994). Though it might not be an absolute state, it enables individuals to be able to respond effectively to ever changing personal, social and economic circumstances. Financial literacy is hypothesised to be a major determinant of the firm's success or failure. It is for this reason, many countries have created task forces to study and evaluate the level of financial literacy of their citizens (Kefela 2010).

With the onset of several financial and economic reforms, the scope of entire market is getting wider. Several new financial products are being introduced in the market generating the need for individuals to plan and invest their finances tactfully. In other words, financial planning is becoming essential for financial well being of an individual. While on the one hand the role of financial planning is largely acknowledged, on the other the significance of financial literacy is still lagging behind, especially for women (Baluja 2016). Moreover, the level of financial literacy among the Indian women has not been widely documented. Hence, the need arises to understand in detail the issue of financial literacy among women in India. This research is an attempt in that direction. It has been observed that although it is imperative that women should be given equal power to take financial decisions as taken by men, yet many Indian women are facing several cultural, financial, psychological and physical barriers that are creating hindrances in their becoming financially literate. The government is taking initiatives for making the people more financially literate, yet there persists a wide gap in the financial literacy level of men and women. Hence, more women specific financial literacy programmes should be introduced and new universities should be established to make women more literate. This would not only make the women more independent and empowered but would facilitate the growth of the whole nation (Kumar and Anees 2013).

In the present scenario, the integrated global financial market as well as the changing financial objectives have increased the individual's responsibility. It would also enable them to manage their own finances and secure their financial future. In an environment where the range and complexity of financial products is widening the scope of entire market, it is becoming crucial for individuals to develop a thorough understanding of the world of finance so as to make better choices, most appropriate to their financial goals and needs (Kumar and Anees 2013). Besides, the economic growth and development of a nation are highly influenced by the financial decisions taken by individuals. However, it is not an easy task to take financial decisions. Several factors such as risk, returns, market scenario and regulatory framework need to be analysed while making financial planning. In other words, financial literacy plays a crucial role in the financial planning of an individual. Financial planning is defined as "the process of meeting one's life goals through the proper management of personal finances" (NISM). In other words, it is a process of taking necessary steps to ensure that an individual is equipped to accomplish their financial goals which they have set out to achieve and is prepared to deal with contingencies as well (Shobha and Shalini 2015). As far as financial literacy is concerned, OECD/INFE defines it as "a combination of awareness, knowledge, skill, attitude and behaviour necessary to make sound financial decisions and ultimately achieve individual financial well- being". Also, it is defined as "the process to inculcate the ability to understand personal financial well-being. It includes the awareness about financial products, market information, sources of getting financial knowledge and confidence of discussing financial issues, so that a person can plan for the future, make proper decisions to meet out the life events" (Migiro 2005). However, everybody does not possess the same ability to plan their financial resources. Researchers across the world have reported the inadequate financial literacy level among the individuals which raises serious concerns about the ability of individuals to secure their financial well-being (Kumar and Anees 2013). There are several factors that actually influence the financial literacy among the individuals and one such prominent factor is 'gender'. More specifically, a relatively broad range of empirical literature documents the existence of gender differences in financial literacy in various countries and along several dimensions. It is generally observed that on an average, women perform worse than men in the tests of financial knowledge and have less confidence in their financial skills (OECD 2013). As far as India is concerned, there have been numerous debates about gender over the years. Mainly such debates are related to women's position in society, their education, health, economic position, gender equality, etc. In other words, women in India have always held a certain paradoxical position. Although the modern society has slowly started recognising her true potential; they are conquering in every field whether politics, sports, entertainment, literature or technology. Yet there are certain areas where women are still lagging behind men. One such area is "personal financial planning". It has been observed that women have inherently been better money managers on a small scale as far as their household expenses and savings are concerned, yet many women, including working women, seem to be comfortable in leaving their long term finances and retirement planning to their fathers or husbands. In other words, the efficiency they exhibit in managing home finances is not getting extended to their personal financial front (Shobha and Shalini 2015). The major reason behind such issue is the lack of financial literacy among women. The survey by NCFE clearly exhibits that the financial literacy percentage among the women in India is quite low which needs special focus (Edwards 2007). Since women form around 50 per cent of the population of India, it would be unjust if only rest of the 50 per cent make the financial decisions. Also, there are several theoretical arguments stating that women should be financially literate to take rationale financial decisions. Some of such arguments are summed up below.

Longer life expectancy

The study by OECD (2013) clearly exhibits that on an average, looking across 121 countries representing a wide mix of the developing and the developed nations, women live five years longer than men. Hence, it is essential that women should develop an in-depth understanding about the concept of financial planning and investment avenues to protect her from the financial challenges she may face in the future. It has been observed in the US, and in cross-national research in the developed countries that older single women continue to be disproportionately poor as compared with older single men and older married couples. Hence, lack of knowledge can be more costly for women because they tend to live longer (*Wall Street Journal*).

Economic growth

The nation's overall development needs women investors as well which will enhance the liquidity in the market and will boost up the scope of trade in the economy. This will be possible if women are financially literate.

Self-reliance

It is essential for women to acquaint themselves with the finance world so as to be financially independent. This will lift up their status in the society as they will match up with the male section of the society as far as financial decisions are concerned.

Freedom from exploitation

Financial literacy will help protect society and individuals against exploitative financial schemes and exorbitant interest rate charged by moneylenders.

Family well-being

It is believed that if there is a difference in the financial literacy level of men and women, it may affect the relative economic power within the household.

Since men and women will allocate household resources according to different preferences, this has implication for the well-being of the family. Research in many countries suggests that households do not act as a single unitary decision maker. Instead, it has been observed that household resources in women's hands are more likely to be spent on improving family well-being, particularly that of children.

However, the exact effect they have on the financial performance of women entrepreneurs has not been fully established by the available literature, hence the need for further research in this area. This study sought to find the factors and degree of financial literacy of woman entrepreneurs. The present study attempts to focus on the existing financial literacy level of woman entrepreneurs in the state of western Odisha. The researcher has examined the association between the demographic and socio-economic profile of entrepreneurs and their financial literacy level. The study also attempts to find whether financial literacy level of woman entrepreneurs has any impact on their investment decision; whether financial literacy level has any association with their monthly expenditure to monthly income ratio and monthly saving to monthly income ratio. The researcher has also identified the factors of financial literacy information most preferred by the entrepreneurs while investing and whether these sources of information did have any influence on investment decision of investors. Given the lack of any clear approach for financial literacy of woman entrepreneurs and baseline data being not available in the Indian context as regards financial literacy level, the present study may provide useful insight into those who are in the field of financial literacy.

Literature review

Financial literacy encompasses the knowledge and skill required by an individual to function effectively in the monetary economy and make informed judgments in respect of their own and their family circumstances. The need for financial literacy among entrepreneurs and business owners has henceforth become an issue of interest in both the developed and the developing economies (Hilgert et al. 2003). Though it might not be an absolute state, it enables individuals to be able to respond effectively to ever changing personal, social and economic circumstances. Financial literacy is hypothesised to be a major determinant of the firm's success or failure. It is for this reason that many countries have created task forces to study and evaluate the level of financial literacy of their citizens (Alessie, Van & Lusardi 2011).

Past literature depicts correlation between financial literacy and financial performance trend of SMEs although the direction of causality is unclear (Hilgert et al. 2003). For instance, according to Bosma and Harding (2006), many SME firms fail because they lack financial literacy, have insufficient business acuity, as well as poor financial literacy, which undermine entrepreneurial activity. Most of the scholars agree that entrepreneurs, regardless of their age, consistently engage in decision-making activities concerning resource procurement, allocation and utilisation. Such activities almost always have financial consequences and thus, in order to be effective, entrepreneurs must be imparted with financial knowledge (Oseifuah 2010). Drexler, Fischer, and Schoar (2014) posited that entrepreneurs usually suffer from insufficient financial literacy to make the complex financial decisions they face. This is unfortunate, since according to Oseifuah (2010), financial literacy among young entrepreneurs contributes meaningfully to their entrepreneurship skills. Entrepreneurs wanting to grow need to be confident of their finances, as well as to be adequately informed (Kinyua 2012). If the owner-managers are illiterate concerning their organisational finances, the financial knowledge of their firms will also be low and this will lead to reduction in innovation that can transform into competitive capability, deprive access to different sources of finance due to non-awareness and this attitude will lead to possible failure of SMEs (Kinyua 2012). In conclusion, entrepreneurs suffer from lack of financial literacy and such deficiency undermines the probability of getting different sources of financing that can result in competitive capability and superior firm performance.

Financial literacy refers to the knowledge of money and financial products that people can apply to financial choices in order to make informed decisions about how to handle their finances (Basu 2005). It includes the ability to make informed judgments and to take effective decisions regarding financial matters (Worthington 2006). OECD (2005) argued that financial literacy must involve not only the investors but also the customers, both having the knowledge of financial products and concepts and their ability to consider financial risks in their decision making and to make other effective actions to improve their financial levels. Financial literacy is essential in helping individuals to identify vital financial issues and behaviours that support effective management of financial resources (Hilgert et al. 2003). It enables one to have the knowledge of critical financial concepts: for instance, types of interests, risks and returns of investments, diversification of investments, among others. Hence it equips them with the ability to understand important financial products needed in life including various bank products, basic investments, ideas and saving plans. It improves how individuals are able to examine and appreciate money and financial issues. This aids greatly in making effective financial decisions with respect to financial management (Lusardi 2004).

Financial literacy not only enables one to make decisions with confidence and sureness, but also assists individuals to respond competently to changes that affect their everyday financial well-being including events in the general economy like collapse of financial markets, rising unemployment and the threat of rapid inflation (Hilgert et al. 2003). Hereafter for any financial system to be effective, financial literacy is required in order to avoid pitfalls and to take appropriate actions to improve the firm's present and future conditions (OCED 2009). Having the numeracy and capacity to do calculations, understanding the financial systems and understanding the risks of financial decisions are some of the fundamental concepts about financial literacy, common measures of financial literacy being basic money knowledge, debt, savings, insurance and investment literacy (Lusardi 2004). As argued by Mandell (2008), there should be more emphasis on raising the level of financial literacy as this would help achieve many objectives of the organisation.

Financial performance refers to the total economic result of activities undertaken by an organisation, whether directly or indirectly (Lusch and Laczniak 1989). It is the efficiency and effectiveness of the organisation (Mandell 2008). Specifically, financial performance of a firm determines how well the business is doing in respect of wealth creation and acquiring of resources (Kumar and Anees 2013) attributes performance to the competency of an organisation to transform the resources within the firm in an efficient and effective manner to achieve organisational goals. To measure financial performance, varied measure approaches have been adopted by various researchers including sales revenue, profits, return on investment/ equity (Wijewardena et al., 2004). The measures include return on sales, combination of RoI and RoS (Pandula 2011) and by its liquidity, which is the amount of cash a company can put its hands on quickly to settle its debts as adopted by Gill (1990). Covin (1991) provides various financial measures which include sales level, sales growth rate, cash flow, return on shareholder equity, gross profit margin, net profit from operations, and ability to fund business growth from profits.

Financial performance mainly influences the firm's growth. Enterprise growth is the unification of quantity and quality. Growth is often closely associated with firm's overall success and survival (Lusardi & Mitchell 2007), hence growth is a measure of performance (Ochieng 2012). Schayek (2011) argues that most of the SME owners or managers are sensitive about disclosing information relating to their firm's financial performance. In addition, Watson (2007) suggests that because most of the SMEs are not required to report and publish their financial records, it is difficult to obtain directly the financial figures on sales and profitability of most of the SMEs. Therefore, most of the research studies such as Lechner, Dowling and Welpe (2006) and Watson (2007) have developed the use of a five-point Likert scale which measures sales growth and profitability growth as financial performance measures. A similar technique is used by Sawyerr et al. (2003), Thrikawala (2011) and Watson (2007). This approach is implemented as it avoids the direct approach of asking for sales or profitability figures but infers the performance indirectly through the responses on the level of satisfaction with sales and profitability growth of the firm. However, it is important to note that sales and profitability growth should not be viewed in isolation as profits and sales may increase as a result of some underlying factor such as price increases or sales promotions respectively, and not due to improved performance of the firm or its products.

Objectives of the study

Following objectives give impetus to the conduct of the present study:

(a) To determine the sources of funding for the businesses owned by the woman entrepreneurs

(b) To find out the relationship of Financial Literacy with Age, Income, Education, Area and other factors among woman entrepreneurs of western Odisha

(c) To find out the most preferred instruments among the respondents

Research methodology

The study was conducted through descriptive and exploratory methods, wherein the researcher has explored the factors and degree of financial literacy level of woman entrepreneurs and then described the impact of the factors by their demographic profile. For the current study, non-probability convenient sampling technique is chosen. The geographical area of the study is confined to Sundargarh and Jharsuguda districts of western Odisha. The two sample districts have been selected on the basis of NDDP (Net District Domestic Product) of *Odisha Economic Survey* 2014 – 15 reports. These two district are coming out with the highest NDDP among the eleven districts of western Odisha.

In the first phase, a pilot study of 17 woman entrepreneurs was conducted. The SD (Standard Deviation) is 1.46, which gives sample size as 57. Data for the study from the 57 sample were collected through self-prepared questionnaire.

The following formula has been used to determine sample size (Nargundkar 2003).

n=(Zσ/e)2

n=(2.575x 1.46/0.5)2 = 56.535 ~57

where,

n= Sample size

Z = Z value from the standard normal distribution for the confidence level desired by the researcher.

For this study, the researcher has assumed 99 per cent confidence level. From the standard distribution tables, the Z value is 2.575; ó = standard deviation of the pilot study. This can be decided by the researcher. For this study, the researcher has assumed the mean population within ± 0.50, n=57

Data analysis

The data pertaining to the demographic profile of the woman entrepreneurs is relevant to the analysis of the understanding of respondents about the perceptions of woman entrepreneurs in western Odisha. The demographic characteristics of the respondents are given in table-1. Majority of the respondents, i.e., 39 (68.4 %) belong to 36 to 45 years of age, and the rest, i.e., 18 (31.6%) are between 26 to 35 years of age. Majority of the woman entrepreneurs belong to general category 42 (73.7%) and 10.5 per cent are OBC and 15.8 per cent SC & ST. Further, maximum of the woman entrepreneurs have income between Rs.10,000 and Rs.20,000. In family type, 57.9 per cent belong to nucleur family and 42.10 per cent to joint family.

Table - 1: Demographic profile of respondents (N = 57)

Particulars	*Frequency*	*Percent*	*Cumulative percent*
Age			
26 to 35 yrs	18	31.6	31.6
36 to 45 yrs	39	68.4	100.0
Total	57	100.0	
Category			
General	42	73.7	73.7
OBC	6	10.5	84.2
SC & ST	9	15.8	100.0
Total	57	100.0	
Monthly income			
Up to Rs. 10,000	18	31.6	31.6
Rs. 10,001 to Rs. 20,000	21	36.8	68.4
Rs. 20,001 to Rs. 30,000	18	31.6	100.0
Total	57	100.0	
Marital status			
Married	57	100.0	100.0
Education			
Up to matric	27	47.4	47.4
10+2	12	21.1	68.4
Graduate	18	31.6	100.0
Total	57	100.0	
Yrs. of entrepreneur			
1 – 5	6	10.5	10.5

(*Contd*...)

6 – 10	42	73.7	84.2
11 – 20	9	15.8	100.0
Total	57	100.0	
Family type			
Nucleus family	33	57.9	57.9
Joint family	24	42.1	100.0
Total	57	100.0	
Category			
First generation entrepreneurs	45	78.9	78.9
Parents as entrepreneurs	3	5.3	84.2
In-laws as entrepreneurs	9	15.8	100.0
Total	**57**	**100.0**	

Also, in the category of enterprise, maximum of women, i.e., 45 (78.9%) are first generation entrepreneurs, followed by "in-laws as entrepreneurs", i.e., 9 (15.8%) and very few have parents as entrepreneurs, i.e., 3 (5.3%).

Table - 2: Sources of finance

Sl. No.	*Particulars*	*Frequency*	*Percent*	*Cumulative per cent*
1.	Own funds only	36	21.1	21.1
2.	Own funds and borrowed funds	135	78.9	100.0
	Total	171	100.0	

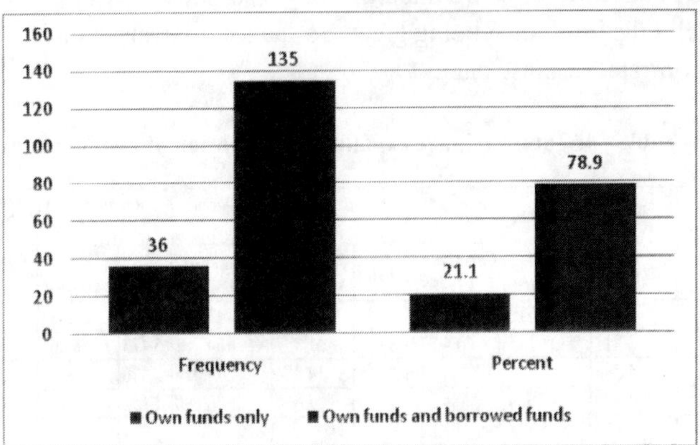

Fig. 1: Sources of finance

The above table and graph represent the source of finance of woman entrepreneurs of western Odisha. The table reveals that 21.1 per cent of entrepreneurs have used their own funds and 78.9 per cent of woman entrepreneurs used their own funds and borrowed funds. This shows that the main sources of finance for woman entrepreneurs are own and borrowed funds.

Analysis of internal homogeneity of items by factor analysis

Factor analysis is applied to 18 variables of motivating women to become entrepreneurs. The KMO value of factor analysis is 0.822 which indicates that factor analysis is reliable for the 18 variables. Also the significance value is coming to 0.000, which also relates the same.

Table - 3: KMO and Bartlett's test

Kaiser-Meyer-Olkin Measure of SamplingAdequacy.		.822
Bartlett's Test of Sphericity	Approx. Chi- Square	308.442
	df	91
	Sig.	.000

Kaiser (1974) recommends values greater than 0.5 as acceptable (values below this should lead to either collect more data or rethink which variable to include). Furthermore, values between 0.5 and 0.7 are mediocre, between 0.7 and 0.8 are good, between 0.8 and 0.9 are great, and above 0.9 are superb. For these data the value is 0.822, which falls into range being great. So, factor analysis is undoubtedly appropriate for these data.

Table - 4: Total variance explained (motivation of respondents)

Component	*Initial eigen values*			*Extraction sums of squared loadings*			*Rotation sums of squared loadings*		
	Total	*% of variance*	*Cumulative %*	*Total*	*% of variance*	*Cumulative %*	*Total*	*% of variance*	*Cumulative %*
1.	7.746	43.035	43.035	7.746	43.035	43.035	5.703	31.684	31.684
2.	3.913	21.737	64.772	3.913	21.737	64.772	5.123	28.464	60.148
3.	2.566	14.254	79.026	2.566	14.254	79.026	3.126	17.366	77.514
4.	1.379	7.664	86.690	1.379	7.664	86.690	1.652	9.176	86.690
5.	.925	5.138	91.828						

(Contd...)

6.	.637	3.541	95.369						
7.	.435	2.419	97.788						
8.	.205	1.138	98.926						
9.	.126	.701	99.627						
10.	.047	.258	99.885						
11.	.021	.115	100.000						
12.	2.46	1.36	100.000						
13.	5E-	9E-	100.000						
14.	16	15	100.000						
15.	1.064E-16	5.913E-16	100.000						
16.	6.010E-17	3.339E-16	100.000						
17.	4.261E-17	2.367E-16	100.000						
18.	######## ######## ########	######## ######## ########	100.000						

Extraction method: Principal component analysis.

Factor analysis is done for all the 18 variables. All these variables have been reduced to four different factors which explains around 86.690 per cent of the total variance. The first factor with its loading pattern indicates that a general factor is running throughout all the items explaining about 31.684 per cent of the variance. The second factor explains about 28.464 per cent, third factor 17.366 per cent and fourth factor explains 9.176 per cent. The entire gamut of five factors explains about 63.196 per cent of the total variance.

Table - 5: Rotated component matrix (Motivation of respondents)

SL.No.	*Variables*	*Component*			
		1	*2*	*3*	*4*
1	Economic independence	-.917	-.267	-.157	**.131**
2	Dissatisfaction with the existing job	**.726**	-.091	.082	.434
3	Unemployment	-.207	-.932	**.747**	-.193
4	Seeking challenge	-.172	**.702**	-.599	-.088
5	Self-interest	**.791**	-.498	-.081	-.269
6	Self-prestige	**.935**	-.307	-.112	.067
7	Traditional / hereditary	-.026	**.887**	-.044	.108
8	Employment opportunities	-.223	.305	**.638**	-.520
9	Financial assistance	.031	-.034	**.961**	.047
10	Technical knowledge	.522	**.809**	.006	.225

(Contd...)

11	Encouragement from family members	.103	**.662**	-.775	.105
12	Use of idle funds	.322	**.798**	.031	-.348
13	Infrastructural facilities	**.959**	.196	.119	.087
14	Entrepreneurial experience	**.967**	.061	-.185	.103
15	Market potentials	**.455**	-.231	.515	-.342
16	Family members interest	.267	.384	**.826**	-.018
17	Social status	.105	.314	.008	**.846**
18	Family background	.425	**.833**	-.019	.084

Extraction method: Principal component analysis.

Rotation method: Varimax with Kaiser normalization.

a. Rotation converged in 6 iterations.

Table - 6: Identification of new parameters by factor analysis

Factors	*Variables*	*New parameters*
Factor 1	Variable 2, 5, 6, 13, 14, 15	Self-esteem
Factor 2	Variable 4, 7, 10, 11, 12, 18	Financial expertise
Factor 3	Variable 3, 8, 9, 16	Financial competency
Factor 4	Variable 1, 17	Economic & social independence

All the 18 variables are reduced to 4 factors. The factors have been extracted through varimax method and through principal component analysis where the eigen value should be greater than 1. Variables 2, 5, 6, 13, 14 and 15 constitute factor-1 which is named as create self-esteem. Variables 4, 7, 10, 11, 12 and 18 constitute factor-2 which is named as financial expertise. Variables 3, 8, 9 and 16 constitute factor-3, named as financial competency. Variables 1 and 17 constitute factor-4 which is named as economic and social independence.

Regression analysis

The concepts and principles developed in dealing with sample linear regression (i.e., one explanatory variable) may be extended to deal with several explanatory variables.

Multiple regression equation

$$Y = C + ßx1 + ßx2 + ßx3 + ßx4 + ßx5 + \dots + ßxn$$

Y = prediction relationship of types of variables with human resource planning

C = Constant value

ß = Unstandardised coefficient

X = Dimension of independent variable

Regression models are used to predict a variable from one or more than one variables. Regression analysis is used to predict the extent of dependence of various factors as its explanatory variable. This was tested by using the first result of the regression analysis, i.e., ANOVA (F-test). Further, R-square value of the regression analysis has been made to show the extent to which the explanatory variables explain the dependent factor.

The second result of the regression analysis, i.e., t-test along with significant value (p-value) indicates the most significant explanatory variable that influences the explained/ dependent factor.

Table - 7: Multiple regression summary output

Regression statistics	
Multiple R	0.989
R-square	0.978
Adjusted R-square	0.984
Standard error	0.020
Observations	100

The R-square value of the above model is 0.978, which means the dependent variable factors motivating women to become entrepreneurs is influenced by all the four explanatory variables: self-esteem, financial expertise, financial competency, economic and social independence by 97.8 per cent, which is a good indicator for establishing well set motivating factors of woman entrepreneurs.

Table - 8: Multiple regression (ANOVA)

	df	*SS*	*MS*	*F*	*Significance F*
Regression	5	19.564	3.913	10139.93	0.000
Residual	93	0.036	0.000		
Total	98	19.600			

Source: Developed from the research.

The ANOVA (F-test) indicates that the scale/factor was quite significant for studying the motivating factors of woman entrepreneurs. All the explanatory variables, i.e., four factors for studying motivating women to become entrepreneurs are quite significant. Further, it is seen from the table that the significant values (p- value) of F-test are 0.000, which means that all four explanatory variables are highly significant with respect to the explained factor, i.e., "factors motivating women to become entrepreneurs". The result is satisfactory as the significance level of the model is less than 0.01. Thus the model used in this research is good.

Table - 9: Multiple regression coefficients

Factors	*Coefficients*	*Standard error*	*t-stat*	*P-value*
Intercept	0.0-02	0.002	-0.998	0.321
Self-esteem (F1)	0.195	0.012	99.327	0.000
Financial expertise (F2)	0.230	0.032	101.809	0.000
Financial competency (F3)	0.210	0.022	100.574	0.000
Economic & social independence (F4)	0.203	0.011	102.183	0.000

Based on the multiple regression output table of "motivating women to become entrepreneurs (Y)" and its constituent variables, the following equation has been derived.

Motivation (Y) = -.002 + 0.195 (F1) + 0.230 (F2) + 0.210 (F3) + 0.203 (F4)

It can be interpreted that the increase of 1 unit of delivery of factor 1 (F1), may incur the raise of 0.195 units in motivating women to become entrepreneurs (Y). The highest Beta indicates that independent variable is the most significant variable in relation to the dependent variable. From table-9 above, the independent factor 2 of 0.230 is the highest among all, meaning that the independent factor 2 contributes the most and has stronger effect on motivating women to become entrepreneurs as compared to other independent variables. Further, it is seen from the table that the significant value (p-value) of t-test for all items is 0.000, which means that all the four factors reduced through factor analysis are highly significant with respect to the explained factor, i.e., "motivating women to become entrepreneurs".

Table - 10: Cross-tabulation of age with monthly expenditure

			Monthly exp.						*Total*
			1% to 50%	*51% to 60%*	*61% to 70%*	*71% to 80%*	*81% to 90%*	*More than 90%*	
Age	26 to 35 yrs .	Count	36	9	0	0	9	0	54
		% within age	66.7%	16.7%	0.0%	0.0%	16.7%	0.0%	100.0%
	36 to 45 yrs .	Count	54	27	9	18	0	9	117
		% within age	46.2%	23.1%	7.7%	15.4%	0.0%	7.7%	100.0%
Total		Count	90	36	9	18	9	9	171
		% within age	52.6%	21.1%	5.3%	10.5%	5.3%	5.3%	100.0%

Table-10 represents the cross-tabulation of age of woman entrepreneurs with their monthly expenditure. The table reveals that woman entrepreneurs in the age of 26 to 35 years have monthly expenditure of 1 to 50 per cent and those in the age of 36 to 45 years have monthly expenditure of 46.2 per cent.

Table - 11: Chi-square tests (age with monthly expenditure)

	Value	*df*	*Sig. (2-sided)*
Pearson chi-square	39.790a	5	.000
Likelihood ratio	51.660	5	.000
Linear-by-linear association	2.517	1	.113
N of valid cases	171		

The chi-square test of age with monthly expenditure reveals that the age of woman entrepreneurs and their monthly expenditure have a significant association. Also, entrepreneurs lower in age are more prone to monthly expenditure and older entrepreneurs are less prone.

Table - 12: Cross-tabulation of age with years of investment

			No. of yrs. of investment			*Total*
			1	*2*	*4*	
Age	26 to 35 yrs	Count	27	27	0	54
		% within age	50.0%	50.0%	0.0%	100.0%
	36 to 45 yrs	Count	45	54	18	117
		% within age	38.5%	46.2%	15.4%	100.0%
Total		Count	72	81	18	171
		% within age	42.1%	47.4%	10.5%	100.0%

Table-12 represents the age of woman entrepreneurs with number of years of investment in saving. The table reveals that older entrepreneurs invest their fund for long periods and vice versa.

Recommendations

The study focused on the motivation of woman entrepreneurs through financial literacy, and recommends that awareness be created among the woman entrepreneurs on the importance of participating in financial literacy training programmes to equip the staff with financial literacy skills. The study also recommends that stakeholders providing financial literacy should consider adding ICT as one of the critical components of training as it opens more sources for raw materials at fair prices. Through technology, businesses can get wider access to markets for their finished products as well as to new and cheap technologies for use in production through the use of the internet.

Conclusion

The findings established that self-esteem, financial expertise, financial competency, economic and social independence are all significant factors motivating women to become entrepreurs. Of all the motivating factors, financial expertise contributes the highest to motivating woman entrepreneurs. Therefore, the study concludes that woman entrepreneurs who are adequately equipped with the above said factors incline more towards entrepreneurship. This is because the skills help them to focus on making personal savings, thus increasing the capital for re-investing and business expansion, which bring in more profits in the long run.

The findings further reveal that woman entrepreneurs' age positively influences monthly expenditure. The study thus concludes that in an industry characterised with more experience, an entrepreneur will be able to stay competitive and maintain well their expenditure level.

The study further concludes that entrepreneurs older in age invest their fund for long periods and vice versa.

10

Case Study on Changing Face of Women Empowerment in India

Soumendra Kumar Patra
Durga Madhab Mahapatra

Abstract

Women-run businesses appear to have mushroomed in most of the cities in the country in recent times. The collective forces of urbanisation and support from government as well as non-governmental organisations have given impetus to women entrepreneurship. This study attempts to assess the impact of entrepreneurship development on women, and reports that venturing into entrepreneurship was taken up as a survival strategy by women. However, it had a positive influence on woman entrepreneurs in terms of self-esteem, self-confidence and decision making leading to their empowerment. The findings indicate that with entrepreneurship development, the respondents developed positive self-esteem as they gained self-confidence and were independent in making their own decisions, thereby reducing their dependence on their spouse/ family members. The income from business had not only made the respondents financially strong, but made them decision makers.

Keywords: *Women, entrepreneurship, empowerment, development, independent, venturing*

Introduction

The standing and role of women and connected issues have attracted the attention of academicians, political thinkers and social scientists in every developing and the developed countries, partially thanks to the observance of the International Women's Decade (1975-85) and partially due to the wide accepted truth that a society designed on the distinction of men and women involves wastage of human resources that no country can afford.

With swelling literature on authorisation of women and with voluminous amount of public expenditure on such schemes, it becomes imperative to know the thought of authorisation of women have a much better understanding of its policy implications.

Women management refers to increasing the spiritual, political, social, academic, gender or economic strength of individuals and communities of women. Women's authorisation in land is heavily hooked on to many variables that embrace geographical location (urban / rural), status (caste and class) and age. Women's property rights are property and inheritance rights enjoyed by women as a category within society at any point in time. The patterns and rights of property ownership vary between societies and are influenced by cultural, racial, political, and legal factors (Agarwal 1994). The lack of control over both productive and non- productive resources that is apparent in both rural and urban settings places women at a reduced level of advantage in areas of security of home, maintaining a basis for survival, and accessing economic opportunities (Agarwal 2005).

Policies on women's authorisation exist at the national, state and native (panchayat) levels in many sectors, along with health, education, economic opportunities, gender - primarily based on violence and political participation. However, there is a gap between policy advancements and actual follow-up at the community level. Empowerment of women is largely the strategy of upliftment of women in economic, social and political spheres. It is a strategy for guarding them against all kinds of violence.

Women authorisation implies a society, a political setting, wherein women can breathe without the fear of oppression, exploitation, apprehension, discrimination and also the general feeling of abuse which are associated with being a woman in a traditionally male dominated structure.

Literature review

In East and South-East Asia, women's participation in work is high. It is possible for women to travel alone relatively late at night. In India, no ITES company can afford to let its woman workers take public transport in the late evening hours, in contrast to reputed multinational competitors - Accenture, IBM, Capgemini, HP, Facebook, and Intel - all of which have had woman chief executives. India's entrepreneurial eco system is rapidly spreading in cities like Bengaluru, Mumbai and Delhi (Varma 2015). However, it must reach smaller towns and villages where people are presented with challenges and opportunities by way of ubiquitous low cost internet connectivity, favourable policies, ease of doing business, affordable education and skilling services, and low cost debt for priority sectors (Prabat 2015). According to *India Skill Report* 2016, an initiative by Wheebox, a global talent assessment company, has come out with ranking done in association with CII, LinkedIn, People Strong and Association of Indian Industries (Varma 2015). According to 2011 census, the work participation rate of women is 25.6 per cent. Equal Remuneration Act 1976 provides for equal remuneration to male and female workers, prevents discrimination on the ground of sex against women in recruitment, promotion, training or transfer, and calls for constitution of advisory committees to enhance employment opportunities for women (Bhattacharya 2015). As per *India Skill Report* 2016, published in *Business Standard,* 28-29 November 2015 (p.12), the top 10 states preferred by women for work are 1. Tamil Nadu 2. Uttar Pradesh 3. Rajasthan 4.Haryana 5. Andhra Pradesh 6.Delhi 7. Gujarat 8. Kerala 9. Karnataka and 10. Punjab, in order of descendence (Verma 2015).

Status of presence of women in different areas

The CSC (Common Service Centre), an internet enabled kiosk set up through the National e-Governance Plan, empowers village level entrepreneurs to provide citizen-centric services including access to land records and utility bill payments. Women run 18 per cent of the 1.4 lakh internet enabled service centres in India today (Bhattacharya 2015). Now India must become a nation of job creators, not just seekers. Becoming an entrepreneur rather than finding a job, must be the aspiration of young people. Market regulator SEBI mandated that companies listed on the bourses not complying with its direction on having at least one woman director on the board will pay a one-time fine of Rs 50,000 during the first 3 months of such non-compliance. According to a recent report, about 12 per cent of over 1,450 companies on the NSE are yet to have a woman director on the board. Around 665 woman directors were appointed to 750 directorship positions (Mishra 2015). Further, towards celebrating motherhood and protecting childhood, the Maternity Benefit Act 1961 permits 12 weeks of leave for employed women (of which 6 weeks immediately after the delivery is mandatory). Similar protection and provisions are extended through Employees State Insurance Act 1948 for establishments not covered under the Maternity Benefit Act 1961 (Wadhwa 2015). The Factories Act 1948, Plantations Labour Act 1951, Contract Labour (Regulation & Abolition) Act 1970, Inter-State Migrant Workmen (Regulation of Employment & Conditions of Service) Act 1979, Beedi and Cigar Workers (Conditions of Employment) Act 1966, Building and Other Construction Workers (Regulation of Employment and Conditions of Services) Act 1996 have certain provisions exclusively for women (Datta 2015). Sexual Harassment of Women at Work-place (Prevention, Prohibition & Redressal) Act 2013 attempts to provide protection against sexual harassment of women and for redressal.

Objectives of the study

The present study was initiated with the following objectives:

(a) To study women empowerment in India

(b) To explore the changing face of women empowerment

(c) To find opportunities for the said case

Research methodology

The study was conducted through Descriptive and Exploratory survey methods, wherein the researcher has explored the different cases of women empowerment with secondary data obtained from different sources. For the current study, the data have been collected from newspapers and print media and consolidated.

Data analysis

Tables-1 and -2 describe the rural and urban sex ratio and work-force participation rate.

Table - 1: Rural-urban distribution of sex ratio

Year	*Rural*	*Urban*
1951	965	860
1961	963	845
1971	949	858
1981	951	879
1991	938	893
2001	946	900
2011	949	929

Source: Office of the Registrar General India, *Business Standard*, 7th December 2015, p. 4.

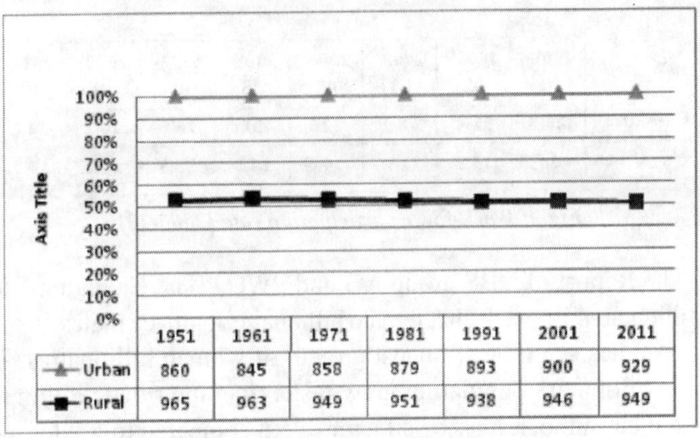

Fig.1: Rural-urban distribution of sex ratio

Table - 2: Work-force Participation Rate (2000 – 12)

Year	*Rural*	*Urban*
2000-01	28.70	14.00
2001-02	31.40	13.90
2002-03	28.10	14.00

(Contd...)

2004-05	32.70	16.60
2005-06	31.00	14.30
2007-08	28.90	13.80
2009-10	26.10	13.80
2011-12	24.80	14.70

Source: BS Research Bureau, *Business Standard*, 7th December 2015, p. 4.

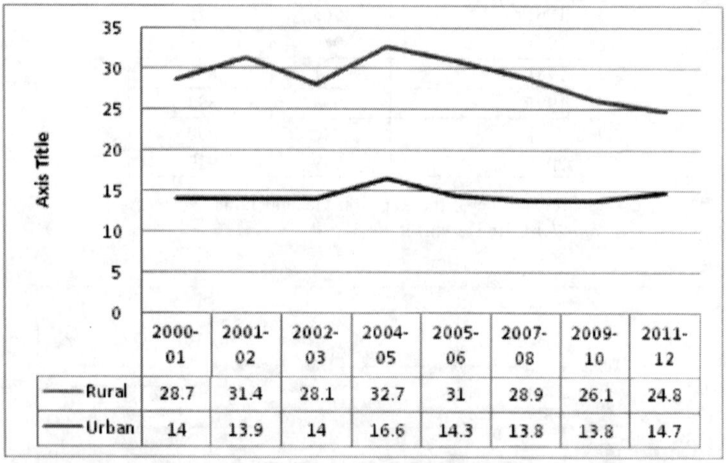

Fig.2: Work-force participation rate (2000-12)

The Report of UBS group AG and PWC, "The Changing Faces of Billionaires", reveals that female billionaires outpace males. It states that Asia has seen the strongest growth of woman billionaires. The female billionaire population grew faster than their male billionaire peers, their number grew by a factor of 6.6 compared to 5.2 for men. Female billionaires are driving their family businesses: 57 per cent in the US, 63 per cent in Europe and 96 per cent in Asia are active wealth creators. The report shows a high attrition rate of billionaires. Only 44 per cent or 126 of 1995's billionaires have prevailed over the last 20 years. The prevailing billionaires grew their assets from an average of USD 2.9 billion to USD 11 billion, outperforming both equity markets and global GDP (https://press.pwc.com/News-releases).

Table - 3: Status of women in politics across the world

Particulars	***Single or lower house***	***Upper house***	***Combined***
Americas	25.2%	25.3%	25.2%
Europe	25.1%	22.8%	24.6%
Sub-Saharan Africa	22.9%	18.9%	22.5%
Asia	18.9%	13.9%	18.4%
Arab States	17.8%	7.7%	16%
Pacific	13.4%	38.6%	16.2%
World	22%	19.5%	21.8%

Source: UNwomen.org 2014, BBC, UN Women, historynet.com, published in *ET Magazine,* p. 15.

Table-3 indicates the status of women in politics across the world. The figures in the table reveal that in lower house America is coming out with the highest percentage (25.2) while in upper house Pacific has the highest percentage (38.6). In combined, America has the highest percentage (25.2) followed by Europe (24.6%). Arab States has the lowest percentage (16.0).

Table - 4: Places with the fewest men per 100 women (2015)

Matinique	84.5
Latvia	84.8
Lithuania	85.3
Curacao	85.6
Guadeloupe	86.0
Ukraine	86.3
Armenia	86.5
Russia	86.8
Belarus	86.8
Estonia	88.0
El Salvador	88.4
Hong Kong	88.5
Portugal	89.9
Arabia	90.6
Hungary	90.8
World	101.8
India	106.1* (As per 2011 Census)

Source: Pew Research Center, *Economic Times,* 22nd Aug. 2015, p.8.

Table-4, representing the places with the fewest men per 100 women in 2015, reveals that India stands the highest among all major countries of the world. Russia and Soviet states have the lowest gender ratios (men per 100 women) in the world.

Table - 5: India's sex ratio vis-a-vis other countries

India	943
Brazil	1031
Russia	1165
China	980
South Africa	1100
Pakistan	942

Note: Figures are based on 2011 census data.
Sex ratio is defined as the number of girls per 1000 boys.

Table - 6: Government of India initiated schemes (2015)

Title	*Amount*	*Objectives*
Beti Bachao Beti Padhao	Rs 100 crore	*Prevention of gender biased sex selective elimination *Ensuring survival and protection of the girl child *Ensuring education and participation of the girl child

Table - 7: Top performing states in terms of sex ratio

States	
Kerala	1084
Tamil Nadu	996
Andhra Pradesh	993
Chhatisgarh	991
Odisha	979

Source: *ET Magazine*, 23-29, Aug. 2015, p.07.

Intel is set to enhance maternity leave benefits to 150 days from the current 84 days or 3 months. The company is also revising its adoption leave policy in line with the enhanced maternity and paternity leave. Intel India recently introduced day-care discount to employees after tying up with a few day care centres. It has increased the representation of women to 20 per cent across much of its 6,900 strong work-force in India and 17 per cent at senior manager and higher levels. Now Intel runs programmes to support advocacy and sponsorship of senior woman employees for their growth and career advancement. These include Intel Network of Executive Women (INEW) and the Asia Network of Executive Women (ANEW). Rapid Orientation for Accelerated Results (ROAR) is another programme aimed at effective integration of newly hired senior woman employees into the company. Table-5 states India's sex ratio vis-a-vis others. Table-7 shows the top performing states in terms of sex ratio. Table-6 describes Government of India initiatives.

Table - 8: Women as percentage of start-up founders worldwide

City	*Percentage*
Chicago	30%
Boston	29%
Sillicon Valley	24%
Los Angels	22%
Montreal	22%
Paris	21%
Tel Aviv	20%
Toronto	19%
Singapore	19%
Kwala Lumpur	19%
London	18%
Moscow	17%

Source: Global Startup Ecosystem, 2015 *ET,* 7 September 2015.

Table-8 presents the number of female entrepreneurs around the world, now significantly higher. According to the Global Startup Ecosystem Ranking 2015, Chicago comes first with women accounting for 30 per cent of new start-ups, with an increase in start-up activities and more number of women taking a plunge into entrepreneurship. Thus, Saha Fund, India's first Securities and Exchange Board of India approved venture capital fund focusing on woman entrepreneurs would have a corpus Rs 100 crore. Woman entrepreneurs face hurdles in finding mentors, get less funding and face perceptual gender bias. At present, India does not have a venture capital fund that exclusively invests in ventures started by woman entrepreneurs. Further, there are a couple of social impact funds, i.e., Sankhya Women Impact Fund, an early stage fund focusing on economically disadvantaged women. Indian women, post-marriage, often relocate to their husband's hometown. In Tier-II and -III cities joint family is still a strong institution and the woman is expected to rely on her immediate relatives. Big growth is happening in e-commerce in women's segment. Flipkart is looking to hire more women candidates, particularly in leadership roles to tap into the key inputs that women can provide in the e-commerce revolution. Further, about 48 per cent of the woman executives under 30 years of age drop out of the work place due to motherhood and related reasons. Flipkart is also working on a proposal to pay 50 per cent of day care charges at high standard facility for children up to 4 years of age. Such a unique maternity policy can cut attrition by 20 to 30 per cent of women and can lead to significant cost saving for the company. Flipkart has introduced women-centric policies with the hope that it will benefit young and expecting mothers who can continue with the same job after a maternity break or post-maternity career break.

Table - 9: Maternity leave provided by different corporate houses in India

Company	*Maternity leaves*
Hindustan Unilever	24 weeks
Godrej	24 weeks
HCL	24 weeks
Accenture	22 weeks
Vodafone	6 months
Flipkart	4 months

Source: Times of India, 2nd July 2015.

Table-9 shows maternity leave provided by different corporate houses in India. The opportunities for women in the Indian Airlines has broader employment opportunities for women. Every year on International Women's Day, March 8, Air India operates a flight on which all operational aspects ground handling, engineering, technical support, even the breathalyser tests for pilots are handled by women. Further, out of 1,100 pilot licences issued in India in 2014 about 170 were to women, an increase of 5 per cent over 2013. In corporate India above, nearly 48 per cent of women drop out of the work force mid-career. The online retailer Big Basket has a strong focus on sexual harassment and it conducts frequent education sessions across company including for women who work in its warehouse. The recent findings of census 2011, the level of women's education in India witnessed a sharp rise between 2001 and 2011, with 116 per cent more of women passing out as graduates or above compared to a just 65 per cent increase among men. Snapdeal has also introduced adoption benefits for male employees who can avail of 3 weeks of leave while female employees can take leave up to 12 weeks after adopting a child. The company has also enhanced its maternity leave from 16 weeks to 25 weeks and paternity leave from 2 weeks to 3 weeks. In addition, new mothers can choose to work from home for 2 months.

Table - 10: Women start-up in India

S.L.	*Name*	*Daughter of*	*Company*
1.	Ananyashree Birla	Kumar Mangalam Birla	Chairperson of Savatantra Microfin.
2.	Shruti Shibulal	SD Shibulal	Director of the Tamara.
3.	Manasi Kirloskar	Vikram Kirloskar	Director of Kirloskar Systems Ltd.
4.	Isha Ambani	Mukesh Ambani	Board of Director of Reliance Jio and Retail Ventures.
5.	Lakshmi Venu	Sundaram Clayton	TVS Group

Table-10 presents a sample of start-ups by women in India. The table reveals that maximum of the top entrepreneurs of big corporate houses are belongs to women.

Table - 11: Women ruling the central banks

SL	Name of Central Bank Governors	Country
1.	Janet Lyellen, Governor of Federal Reserve, since Feb. 2014	
2.	Elvira Nabiullina, Governor, Central Bank since 2013	Russia
3.	Zeti Akhtar Aziz, Governor, Central Bank in 2000	Malaysia
4.	Tarisa Watanagase, Governor since 2006	Thailand
5.	Gill Marcus, Governor, Central Bank , Nov. 2009	South Africa

Source: Bloomberg, *Financial Times,* Forbes, National Central Bank.

Table - 12: Percentage of female teachers 1990 - 2016

S.L.	*Country*	*Primary education*	*Secondary education*
1.	Russia	98.8	82.1
2.	Brazil	89.6	65.2
3.	South Africa	78.4	54.8
4.	Indonesia	62.1	53.1
5.	China	61.0	51.0
6.	South Asia	49.5	42.4
7.	India	48.2	45.1

Data years 2016, 2015.
Source: ET, 7 Oct. 2016, p.12.

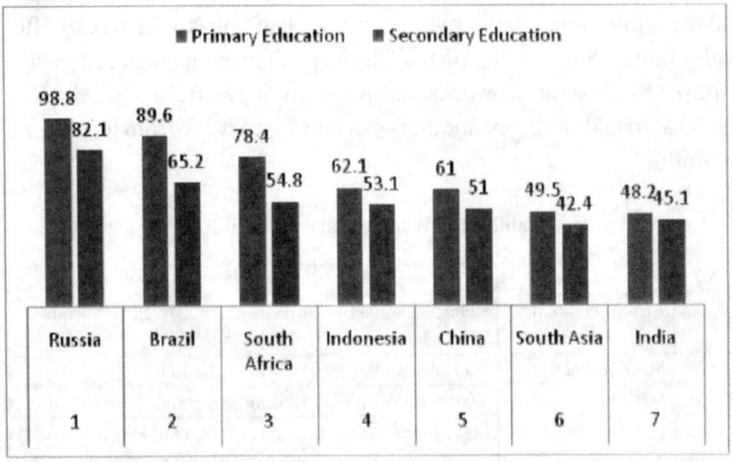

Fig. 3: Percentage of Female Teachers 1990 - 2016

The table and chart shows the percentage of woman teachers in primary and secondary education in India and outside. The figure shows that the proportion of woman teachers in both is comparatively good in numbers. However, among the figures of outside India, Russia has the the highest number followed by Brazil.

Opportunities

1. Most married women in India avoid making financial decisions. A 2013 survey by Ameriprise Financial reveals that many women stay out of money matters to avoid marital discard.

2. Ericsson, the world's number one telecom equipment maker, has been aggressively hiring women in its core operations in India. The women engineers in Ericsson India will, for the first time, be involved in main line consulting and systems integration, 3G and 4G network roll-outs, network design and optimisation, etc.
3. Indian IT Services Company at present has a woman in top position. Accenture has named Reha M. Menon its chairman for India. IBM India has Vanitha Narayana as its Managing Director, while Intel India is headed by Kumud Srinivasan as president and Capgemini India is headed by chief executive Aruna Jayanthi. Similarly, HP India is headed by Neelam Dhawan as managing director and at Facebook India managing director Kirthiya Reddy heads the social networks operations in the country. TCS elevated Arathi Subramanian, head of its global delivery excellence group; ITC Infotech, the wholly owned IT outsourcing subsidiary of ITC group appointed Sushma Rajgopalan as CEO and MD in ITC Infotech elected to the NOA council 2016.
4. Now banks want more women in the trading room, technology and several other roles generally dominated by men. Gender diversity is a business led initiative. Chanda Kochhar is the only woman on the ICICI bank board. Sikha Sharma is the only woman on the executive committee at the Axis Bank. Further, Naina Lal Kidwai is the executive director on the board of HSBC, Asia-Pacific and Chairman of HSBC India. Another six women at the top at Deutsche Bank are Sandhya Vasudevan, COO; Anjali Mohanty, head of global transaction business; Radha Dhir, Head of Corporate Banking; Anjaallee Paatil, Head Legal; Radhika Kamat, Head Taxation; and Madhavi Lal, Human Resources.

Conclusion and discussion

Understanding empowerment in this way means that development agencies cannot claim to empower women, rather they provide appropriate external support and intervention which may, however, be important to fostering and supporting the process of empowerment, i.e., they may act as facilitators. Governments can ensure that their programmes work to support women's individual empowerment by encouraging women's participation, acquisition of skills, decision making capacity, and control over resources. Therefore, an inclusive approach whereby the planners should work towards empowerment must develop ways of enabling women themselves to critically review their own situation and participate in creating and shaping the society.

11

Impact of Entrepreneurial Traits of SHG Members on Women Empowerment

Seema Ghosh

Abstract

The achievement of human development is dependent on the development and empowerment of women. Women entrepreneurship, women empowerment and nation building are synonymous. The purpose of this study is to identify the entrepreneurial traits among the self-help group women and the impact of their entrepreneurial traits on women empowerment. The entrepreneurial traits explored are risk taking ability, need for achievement, confidence and determination to succeed. The study uses principal factor analysis to assess the entrepreneurial traits of self-help group women. The research is based on primary data collected in the Medak district of Telangana state, using structured questionnaire with Likert scale. Simple regression analysis is used to examine the relationship between entrepreneurial traits and women empowerment. Hierarchical regression analysis was applied to study the role of entrepreneurial traits as a moderator between financial intermediation and women empowerment.

Keywords: *Women empowerment, entrepreneurial traits, self-help group women.*

Background

The achievement of human development is dependent on the development and empowerment of women. Their socio-economic development forms the basis for sustainable growth of the economy. The Constitution of India guarantees the right of equality to all citizens for sustainable development of all. There are about 580 lakh women in India today, and 400 lakh of them live in villages. While women represent 48 per cent of the total population of India, they constitute only 31 per cent of the employment market. Of this population, 91 per cent are employed in unorganised sector. The rural woman labour force participation rate in unorganised sector stands at per cent. (Report of the Committee on Unorganized Sector Studies: 2012). Gender inequality in India persists despite high rates of economic growth. Participation of women in employment and decision-making remains far lower than that of men. India's poor performance in women's empowerment and gender equality is reflected in many indicators, the most telling of which is the sex ratio which has, in some parts of India, dropped to 833 females per 1000 males. Gender inequality is also reflected in India's low rank on the Gender Inequality Index, which is 127 out of 151 countries, with a value of 0563. The Gender Inequality Index measures the inequality in terms of achievements between males and females in three main aspects namely labour market, reproductive health and empowerment (UN Human Development Report: 2013).

There is global recognition for women's contributions to economic development. Empowering women is one of the Millennium Development Goals of the United Nations. This is because it is recognised that women empowerment brings about other developmental processes associated with it. Empowerment is a process that results in the expansion of women's agency, i.e., in their ability to make choices affecting their lives and situations (Malhotra et al. 2002).World Bank (2001) reports that societies in which gender discrimination prevails poverty is greater, governance weaker and standard of living lower. Therefore investing in women has a greater multiplier effect in terms of their ability to transform their lives and situations through financial access. The access of financial resources presents an opportunity for greater empowerment of women. In India, the concept of self-help group has been evolved as a key instrument to deliver micro credit to poor rural women to undertake the entrepreneurial activities. There have been numerous examples of how women in rural areas have been able to become financially self-reliant through self help groups route.

Review of literature

Over the last two decades, SHG programme in India has become an important tool for alleviating poverty. The SHG programme focuses on delivering financial and non- financial facilities to its members through micro credit, savings, insurance and other financial and non-financial services. Prof. Yunus of Bangladesh introduced the concept of micro credit for the first time among the poor women in 1976 in Bangladesh under the Grameen Bank. In India, the programme involving financial intermediation was launched in 1992 by NABARD as the SHG-bank linkage programme. The programme had started as a link between the unbankable rural poor and the formal banking system to cater to the micro credit needs of the poor. Today, the SHG-bank linkage programme stands as the world's largest micro finance initiatives with over 74 lakh SHGs representing 970 lakh rural households directly becoming part of the programme (NABARD Report: 2014).

Self-help group (SHG) is a self-governed, controlled and small informal association of the poor, usually from socio-economically homogeneous families who are organised around savings and credit activities (National Commission for Women 2004). Most SHGs are women groups with membership ranging between 10 and 20. SHGs are development groups for the poor and the marginalised who come together to save and access credit. The purpose of the SHG is to build the financial capacity of the poor and the marginalised in the field of employment and income generating activities. They have well defined rules and by-laws, hold regular meetings and maintain records of savings and credit discipline. They are a self-managed institution characterised by participatory and collective decision-making. They are recognised by the government and do not require formal registration (Planning Commission 2008).

In India, SHG linkage programme has been promoted by the government agencies and non-government agencies (NGOs). The fundamental objective of this programme is to create self-employment opportunity for the rural women and thus enhance their income earning capacity. The income generating activities facilitate the increasing of household income that improves the consumption pattern and lifestyles of their families (Navajas et al. 2000).The SHG also encourages women borrowers to save from their profits for their future expansion. The involvement of rural women in income generating activities also benefits in bringing a change in their attitudes with regard to education, consumption, health and sanitation (Afrin et al. 2008).

Women empowerment is the other main purpose of SHG intervention. The essence of empowerment can be examined on three aspects. Firstly, as an expansion of agency which indicates focus on the individual by providing them skills, confidence, self- respect and information so that they become an agent of change. Secondly, it intends to include institutional environment which offers people the opportunity to exert the agency fruitfully. Thirdly, it operates as an on-going process for expansion rather than simply as an end product (Mosedale 2003). The outcome of the SHG programme can be explained in two dimensions. Firstly, the programme assists in creating employment opportunity, improving the economic status, providing economic security, building assets and generating wealth for the rural families (Puhazhendhi and Badatya 2002). Secondly, the SHG programme also brings the impact on social empowerment, awareness and education, self-esteem, sense of dignity, organisational and management skills, mobilisation of collective strengths, etc. (Pitt and Khandaker 1996). The positive socio-economic impact helps the rural women to come out of the vicious circle of poverty and indebtedness and become more financially stable.

Entrepreneurship is a prerequisite for the development of any nation. It is the risk taking ability of the individual with correct decision-making. It is a composite skill, the resultant of a mix of many qualities and traits. If the personal characteristics of an individual are typical of an entrepreneurial personality, then those individuals are potential entrepreneurs (Macmillan 1988, as cited in Nishanthi 2014). According to Schumpeter (1949), innovation is the main characteristics of an entrepreneur. "The carrying out of new combinations call enterprise and the individuals whose function is to carry them out call entrepreneurs". Ahmed (1982) highlights risk taking capability as an essential characteristic of an entrepreneur. Aperson is entrepreneurial when he or she has very strong eagerness to achieve (McClelland 1961). The motivation to achieve also is an important characteristic of an entrepreneur. The entrepreneur is the individual or team that identifies the opportunity, gathers the necessary resources, creates and is ultimately responsible for the performance of the organisation. As a catalysing agent, the entrepreneur creates the forces of change and utilises the same in accelerating the socio-economic value addition of a country through utilisation, employment generation, capital accumulation and industrialisation (Rahman 1979, as cited in Afrin et al. 2008). Siroplos (1994) has identified six major traits that an entrepreneur should possess. They are creativity and innovation, risk taking, self-confidence, hard working, goal setting and accountability (as cited in Nishanthi 2014).

Research problem

The main objective of women empowerment is to broaden the scope of income generating activities and enhance the reach of the financial system that can tap the fortune at the bottom of the pyramid (Prahlad 2009). Entrepreneurship enhances financial empowerment and self-esteem of women. Financial inclusion is integral to the process of women empowerment and sustainable development of the country (Sreeramulu 2006). Economic independence of the poor people is the key driver towards eradicating poverty and inequality (Mujumdar 2008). Micro finance through self-help groups has emerged as a viable means of economic empowerment of women. The provision of credit to poor women is instrumental to bringing about socio-cultrual, economic and political empowerment (Ramakrishna 2010). Rural women are benefited from the credit provided by the SHGs for their income generating activities and have become self-reliant and economically empowered. However, it is difficult to identify the contribution made by entrepreneurial traits of the SHG women which probably assist them to sustain their economic activities and thus influence empowerment. In this situation, this study primarily focuses on assessing the impact of financial intermediation services of SHGs on women empowerment. It also analyses the role of entrepreneurial traits as a moderator between financial intermediation services provided by SHG on women empowerment. The specific objectives of the study are as follows:

1. To assess the impact of financial intermediation services of SHGs on women empowerment
2. To analyse the impact of entrepreneurial traits of self-help group members on women empowerment
3. To study the efficacy of entrepreneurial traits as a moderator between financial intermediation and women empowerment.

Hypotheses

In this study, the following hypotheses have been developed:

H1: Financial intermediation services of self-help groups have a positive impact on women empowerment.

H2: Entrepreneurial traits of self-help group women have a positive impact on women empowerment.

H3: Entrepreneurial traits of self-help group women moderate the relationship between financial intermediation services and women empowerment.

Research methods

The research is based on primary data collection in the Medak district of Telangana state. The selection of Medak district was based on the criteria of its geographical location, its industrial proximity to the capital city of Hyderabad and the opportunity there to start a micro enterprise. For the study, 150 self-help group women who were involved in running a micro enterprise in their villages were randomly selected. The data was collected by distributing the structured questionnaire consisting of closed ended questions to the respondents. The items in the questionnaire were targeted to measure the key variables of the study. The respondents were requested to rate the statements on each variable dimension on a 5- point likert scale ranging from "1: strongly disagree to 5: strongly agree". The internal consistency and reliability were established for the study by the method of Cronbach alpha, and the alpha coefficient obtained was 0.86. This study analyses two independent variables, namely financial intermediation services and entrepreneurial traits of SHG women and their impact on women empowerment. It also studies the role of entrepreneurial traits as a moderator between financial intermediation and women empowerment. The criteria for selecting suitable indicators for measuring women empowerment are taken from the study of Sabina and Solava (2007). According to the study, firstly, the selected indicators should assess the intrinsic aspects of agency and empowerment. Secondly, the indicators should identify the change in empowerment levels over time. Thirdly, the selection of the indicators should also be in line with the indicators, which are often used in research to adequately measure empowerment. Based on the above criteria, the study selected a set of indicators of empowerment. Women empowerment was operationalised using 15 items measuring five factors of autonomy on the expenditure, control over the loan, ownership of assets, participation in decision- making and improvement in self-confidence.

The core start for identifying the traits of anentrepreneur comes from the identification of the Big Five broad category of personality traits which was developed by Costa and McCrae (1987). The broad measures have been used to identify the traits of an entrepreneur, often attributed to the success of small businesses (Kiggundu 2002). The entrepreneurial traits identified are the traits of small and medium business owners. The measurement of the entrepreneurial traits in the study is adopted from Sorensen and Chang (2006) and Blackman (2003). The study consists of three factors of entrepreneurial traits namely risk taking ability, need for achievement, confidence and determination to succeed measured using 12 items. In India, self-help groups are promoted by government agencies, non-government organisations (NGOs) or banks. The major programme involving financial intermediation by SHGs is the SHG-bank linkage programme launched by NABARD. Apart from NABARD, there are micro finance institutions (MFIs) providing credit to SHGs. The groups manage and lend their accumulated savings and externally leveraged funds to their members. The financial intermediation services in the study are measured via 11 items indicating financial intermediation services and financial intermediation system.

Along with descriptive statistics, multi-variate analysis techniques such as factor analysis, correlation, multiple regression analysis and hierarchical regression analysis were used to analyse the factors influencing women empowerment and the interaction effect. A Principal Factor Analysis with an orthogonal rotation (Varimax) using the SPSS statistical package was used to separate the factors for independent and dependent variables. The impact of independent variables (financial intermediation services and entrepreneurial traits of SHG women) on the dependent variable (women empowerment) was tested through multiple regression. The moderating effect between entrepreneurial traits and financial intermediation services was assessed through hierarchical multiple regression analysis as described by Barron and Kenny (1986). Financial intermediation services were entered in step 1, entrepreneurial traits in step 2 and the interactive term (financial intermediation * entrepreneurial traits) in step 3 to predict women empowerment. All the predicting variables were median centred prior to multiplication in order to reduce multi- collinearity.

Descriptive statistics

The respondents of the study were rural women engaged in running a micro enterprise in their villages of Medak district of Telengana state. The total number of SHG women interviewed was 150. Of them 45 per cent were in the age group of 30 to 40 years, followed by 40 to 50 years (20%), 20 to 30 years (15%), 50 to 60 years (15%) and above 60 years (5%). The average age of the SHG women respondents was 30 years. While 85 per cent of the SHG women respondents were married, 15 per cent were widows. The educational qualification status of the rural SHG women respondents shows that 42.5 per cent of them were illiterates, 35 per cent had completed middle school, 12.5 per cent completed high school, 5 per cent had intermediate and another 5 per cent were graduates. All respondents had been the members of SHG for an average period of 10 years and they had availed loan facility from their respective SHG to start a micro enterprise, which they were running successfully. These rural women were involved in operating small enterprises for making pickles agarbatis, pickles, powder, soaps, detergents, footwear, bamboo products, etc. The loan amount taken by the respondents ranged from a minimum of Rs. 5,000 to a maximum of Rs. 80,000. Almost all the women had taken loan more than once from their SHG.

Results

Multi-variate Analysis technique such as factor analysis was used to identify and explain the factors responsible for women empowerment with the support of micro credit. A Principal Factor analysis using SPSS package was administered to the study data to separate the factors for each independent and dependent variable. Factor analysis of 11 variables in the financial intermediation services data identified two main factors that accounts for 74.28 per cent of the variance as shown in table-1. The first factor identified as financial intermediation services accounted for 57.41 per cent of the variance in the data. The eigen value of this factor is 6.80 (table-1). Financial intermediation services factor was related to five variables such as fair interest charged on loans (0.908), sufficient duration of loan (0.932), compulsory monthly savings (0.827), compulsory monthly repayment of loan (0.835) and flexibility in repayment of loan (.898). The communality values for these variables were 0.840, 0.889, 0.685, 0.818, and 0.811 respectively (table-2). Similarly, the second factor identified as financial intermediation system accounted for 16.87 per cent of the variance in the data. The eigen value of this factor is 1.363 (table-1). Financial intermediation system factor is related to six variables such as effective and efficient system (0.813), sufficient and sustainable lending (0.774), time taken for sanction (0.673), procedure for obtaining loan (0.797), terms and conditions for loans (0.724) and overall working of the system (.867). Arelatively higher level of factor loading of almost all variables indicates that these variables were very important to constituting the two factors. The communality values for these variables are 0.708, 0.669, 0.521, 0.797, 0.673 and 0.760 respectively (table-2). The higher level of communality of the variables associated to the factors indicates that each variable is very much related to the respective factor. The KMO and Bartlett's test result is 0.798, which supports the factor analysis.

Table - 1: Financial intermediation services factors

Name of the factor	*Eigenvalue*	*Cumulative variance (%)*
Financial intermediation services	6.80	57.41
Financial intermediation System	1.363	74.28

Table - 2: Factor dimensions and factor extraction: Financial intermediation services

	Initial	*Extraction*
Factor 1- Financial intermediation services		
There is a fair interest rates charged on loans	1.000	.840
The duration of loan provided is sufficient	1.000	.889
I am comfortable with compulsory monthly saving	1.000	.685
I am comfortable with compulsory monthly repayment of loan	1.000	.818
There is flexibility in repayment of loan	1.000	.811
Factor 2 – Financial intermediation System		
There is an effective and efficient system for providing loans	1.000	.708
The SHG ensures sustainable and sufficient lending	1.000	.669
The time taken for sanctioning of is reasonable	1.000	.521
The procedure for obtaining loan is easier than banks	1.000	.797
I have information on the terms and condition on loans	1.000	.673
I am satisfied with overall working of the system	1.000	.760

Extraction method: Principal Component Analysis.
Source – Primary data.

Tables-3 and-4 present the result concerning factor analysis of entrepreneurial traits of SHG women constituted by three factors accounting for 72.37 per cent of the variance. The three factors are risk taking ability, confidence and determination and need for achievement with eigen value of 4.58, 2.93 and 1.17 respectively. Each factor explains 38.18 per cent, 21.44 per cent and 12.75 per cent variance respectively. The risk taking ability is concerned with meeting targets (0.815), function in ambiguous situation (0.715), borrowed money from other sources (0.789) and expansion of business (0.732). Confidence and determination factor is explained by communicate convincingly (0.914), willingness to do even when people laugh (0.843), ability to understand (0.734) and quick decisions (0.858). The variables forming the need for achievement factor include improvement by training (0.559), 50 hours work (0.839), optimistic about business (0.635) and learn new aspects (0.575). The KMO and Bartlett's test result is 0.710, which supports the factor analysis. A relatively higher factor loading indicates the importance of these variables for determining all the factors of functioning of SHG and entrepreneurial traits. The communality of the variables is also higher.

Table - 3: Entrepreneurial traits factors

Name of the factor	*Eigenvalue*	*Cumulative variance (%)*
Risk taking ability	4.58	38.18
Confidence and determination	2.93	59.62
Need for achievement	1.170	72.37

Source – Primary data.

Table - 4: Factor dimensions and factor extraction: Entrepreneurial traits

	Initial	*Extraction*
Factor 1- Risk taking ability		
I am able to meet targets	1.000	.822
I can function in ambiguous situation	1.000	.621
I have borrowed money from other sources to invest in the business	1.000	.698
I have expanded business over a period of time	1.000	.709
Factor 2– Confidence and determination		
I can communicate convincingly with others like bankers, vendors	1.000	.861
I am willingness to do something even when other people laugh	1.000	.734
I have ability to understand the market for my product	1.000	.806
I can make decision quickly	1.000	.786
Factor 3– Need for achievement	1.000	.558
I have improved on training and knowledge for business	1.000	.722
I am willing to work more than 50 hours per week	1.000	.666
I am optimistic about my business I have interest to learn new aspects about business	1.000	.703

Extraction method: Principal Component Analysis. Source – Primary data.

Tables-5 and-6 demonstrate the result of factor analysis of women empowerment, the dependent variable. This is explained by five factors such as autonomy on expenditure, control over the loan, ownership of assets, participation in decision- making and improvement in self-confidence. The factors accounts for 74.23 per cent of the variance. Individually each factor has 20.37 per cent, 17.99 per cent, 12.67 per cent, 12.08 per cent and 11.12 per cent variance with eigen value of 3.50, 2.43, 1.58, and 1.07. Three variables constitute the factor autonomy on expenditure such as freedom to spend (0.808), spend money for festivals (0.820) and spending on health (0.695). Control over loan factor is explained by discretion to use loan amount (0.576), able to pay interest (0.658) and repayment on time (0.810). The variables owner of assets (0.695) and co-owner of assets (0.973) constitute the factor ownership of assets. The variables forming the factor participation in decision- making include decision making for the purchase of assets (0.725), decision-making on the additional expenses (0.624) and financial decision-making (0.794). Improvement in self-confidence factor was constituted by four variables, namely improvement in household status (0.795), improvement in social status (0.669), involvement in community programmes (0.753) and confidence to voice concern (0.744). Higher factor loading indicates the importance of the variables constituting a factor and higher communality shows the relevance of each variable to the factor. The KMO and Bartlett's test result is 0.717, which supports the factor analysis.

Table - 5: Women empowerment factors

Name of the factor	*Eigen value*	*Cumulative variance(%)*
Autonomy on Expenditure	3.50	20.37
Control over the loan	2.43	38.36
Ownership of assets	1.58	51.03
Participation in decision making	1.37	63.11
Improvement in self confidence	1.07	74.23

Source – Primary data.

Table - 6: Factor dimensions and factor extraction: Women empowerment

	Initial	*Extraction*
Factor 1 – Autonomy on expenditure		
I have freedom to spend to buy for monthly provision	1.000	.723
I generally spend money for festivals, customs etc	1.000	.694
If required, the expenses on health are met by me	1.000	.595
Factor 2 – Control over the loan		
I have the discretion to use loan amount	1.000	.763
I am able to pay the interest on loan	1.000	.763
I repay the loan on time	1.000	.753
Factor 3 – Ownership of assets		
I have become owner of assets	1.000	.736
I have become co owner of assets	1.000	.836
Factor 4 – Participation in decision making		
I participate in decision making for the purchase of assets	1.000	.723
I participate in decision making on the additional expenses on festival and others	1.000	.692
I am involved in financial decision making regarding renovation of house, sanitation	1.000	.737
Factor 5 –Improvement in self confidence		
There is an improvement in household status	1.000	.738
There is an improvement in social status	1.000	.683
I am actively involved in community programs like health, sanitation, girl development etc	1.000	.883
I have confidence to voice my concern in social community	1.000	.798

Extraction method: Principal Component Analysis.
Source – Primary data.

Model specification

Multiple regression model is used to establish the relationship and magnitude between financial intermediation services (FIS) and entrepreneurial traits of SHG women (ET) as independent variable and women empowerment (WE) as dependent variable. Therefore the model used in the study is:

$$WE = \alpha + \beta 1\ FIS + \beta 2\ ET + \varepsilon$$

Where;

α = intercept, $\beta 1$, $\beta 2$ = coefficient of independent variable, ε = error term

Pearson correlation coefficient is used to determine the strength and direction of association between financial intermediation services, entrepreneurial traits of SHG women and women empowerment. The results in Table 7 shows all correlations are significant ($p < 0.01$). The correlation coefficient 0.833 and 0.643 shows a positive relationship between financial intermediation services and entrepreneurial traits of SHG women as independent variables and women empowerment as dependent variable.

Table - 7: Correlations

Variables	*Women empowerment*	*Entrepreneurial traits*	*Financial intermediation*
Women empowerment	1		
Entrepreneurial traits	.643(**)	1	
Financial intermediation	.833(**)	.655(**)	1

** Correlation is significant at the 0.01 level (2-tailed). Source: Primary data.

Table-8 presents the result of multiple linear regression. The result establishes significant effect of financial intermediation services and entrepreneurial traits of SHG women on women empowerment with $R2 = 0.617$, $F = 33.939$, $p < 0.01$. The independent variables together explain 61.7 per cent variance of women empowerment. The coefficient of financial intermediation services and entrepreneurial traits of SHG women are 0.425 and 0.078 respectively. They are all positive, meaning that as the magnitude of independent variable increases the magnitude of dependent variable also increases. Financial intermediation services of SHG have the high beta ($\beta = 0.425$), which implies that the financial intermediation services of SHG have a strong influence on women empowerment. Entrepreneurial traits of SHG women with $\beta = 0.078$ has a positive impact on women empowerment but statistically insignificant. This suggests that entrepreneurial traits by themselves may not have any meaningful impact on women empowerment.

Table - 8: Multiple regression results

Dependent variable: Women empowerment Independent variable		
	Constant	0.184
1.	Financial intermediation	0.425 *
2.	Entrepreneurial traits	0.078***
	R square	0.639
	Adj. R square	0.617
	F	33.939**

Notes- **p < 0.01, p*< 0.05 (Standard beta coefficients), p*** = 0.502.
Source – Primary data.

Table-9 demonstrates the results concerning the moderating effects. The results show that the interaction of financial intermediation and entrepreneurial traits significantly and positively influences women empowerment (D = 0.408, p <0.05). The interactive term makes a significant contribution to R2 (DR2 = 0.043, p < 0.05). This finding indicates that the impact of interaction of financial intermediation and entrepreneurial traits is significant.

Table - 9: Hierarchical multiple regression results: moderating effects

Dependent variable: Women empowerment			
Independent variable	Step 1	Step 2	Step 3
Constant	____	____	____
1. Financial intermediation	0.824 **	0.710 **	0.422*
2. Entrepreneurial traits		0.174***	0.086****
3. FI * ET		0.408*	
R square	0.579 0.596	0.639	
Adj. R square	0.571	0.580 0.618	
Change R square	0.579 0.017	0.043	
F change	80.390**	2.105* 5.936*	

**p <0.00 , *p < 0.05 (Standard beta coefficients), ***p = 0.155 , ****p = 0.471
FI*ET – financial intermediation* entrepreneurial traits.

Source: Primary data.

Discussion and conclusion

The present study developed and tested a model that examined financial intermediation services provided by SHG and entrepreneurial traits of SHG women as the factors that influence women empowerment. The model also tested entrepreneurial traits of SHG women as a moderator of the impact of financial intermediation service on women empowerment. The SHG women owning and running their own micro enterprises in Medak district of Telengana state served as the sample of the study. The results of the study are based on the colleted primary data. The overall conclusion from the findings of the study was that the hypotheses gained acceptance from empirical data. The results are consistent with the findings of Aragaw (2011), and Gaurang and Sandeep (2011).

In hypothesis-1 (H1), it was predicted that financial intermediation services have a direct and positive relationship with women empowerment. The result in this study suggests that the impact of financial intermediation services of self-help groups on women empowerment is positive and significant ($\beta = 0.425$, $p < 0.05$). This means that if rural women get credit support from SHG, they can take the initiative of establishing some small business, which will help them to be economically and socially empowered. This result indicates that, greater the financial intermediation services provided by SHG, greater is the chance of women being more empowered.

In hypothesis-2 (H2), it was predicted that entrepreneurial traits of self-help groups have a direct and positive effect on women empowerment. This indicates that if rural SHG women can manage their micro enterprises successfully, then it is their individual entrepreneurial traits which help them to become empowered. The result shows a positive impact on women empowerment with $\beta = 0.078$, $p = 0.502$ which is statistically insignificant. This suggests that entrepreneurial traits on their own may not have any meaningful impact on women empowerment.

With regard to hypothesis 3 (H3), it was perceived that entrepreneurial traits of self-help group women act as a moderator between financial services and women empowerment. This indicates that if a rural womAn has the facility to access funds from the self-help group and establish a micro enterprise, the individual entre-preneurial traits enhance the possibility for her to run and sustain the business successfully and profitably. The result indicates that entrepreneurial traits as a moderator between the relationship of financial intermediation services and women empowerment is significant ($\beta = 0.408$, $p < 0.05$). The interaction of financial intermediation services and entrepreneurial traits contributes significantly to R2 (DR2= 0.043, $p < 0.05$). This suggests that entrepreneurial traits moderate between financial intermediation services and women empowerment.

It is observed and recognised that the self-help group initiative has assisted rural women to be economically and socially empowered. It has improved the socio- economic status of rural women. It is also ascertained that credit facility by SHG supports the rural women to become entrepreneurial. This study tried to explain that entrepreneurial traits of SHG rural women could impact women empowerment by constructing a model, which was şupported by the multi-variate analysis. The finding of the study is that financial intermediation services of SHG and entrepreneurial traits of rural SHG women have a positive and significant relationship with women empowerment. The significant relationship indicates that the financial intermediation services of SHG have the ability to empower women economically and socially. When the rural women receive the financial support from SHG, they are encouraged to involve in income generating activities. The individual entrepreneurial traits enhance their chances to run and sustain the business successfully and profitably. Apart from financial loans, SHGs should focus on providing assistance and support to their members for managing and running their micro enterprises successfully and profitably, and making the rural women really empowered.

The present study had some limitations, as there are many other factors which affect women empowerment apart from the factors taken into consideration in the study. Consequently, the applicability of results is partially true. Moreover, the study analyses the role of entrepreneurial traits as a moderator between financial intermediation and women empowerment. Other variables that are important in the relationship can also be explored.

Bibliography

Afrin, S., Islam, N., & Ahmed, S.U. (2008). A Multivariate Model of Micro Credit and Rural Women Entrepreneurship Development in Bangladesh, *International Journal of Business and Management, 3*(8), 169-185. doi: http://dx.doi.org/10.5539/ijbm.v3n8p169

Agarwal, B. (1994). Gender and Command over Property: A Critical Gap in Economic Analysis and Policy in South Asia, *World Development, 22*(10), 1455-1478. doi: https://doi.org/10.1016/0305-750X(94)90031-0

Agarwal, B. (2005). Marital Violence, Human Development and Women's Property Status in India, *World Development, 33*(5): 823–850. doi: https://doi.org/10.1016/j.worlddev.2005.01.009

Ahmed, S.U. (1982). Entrepreneurship and Economic Development, Dhaka University Studies, Part-C, 3(1), 41-53.

Allahabad, M.-D. (n.d.). District Industrial Profile of Sant Ravidas Nagar (Bhadohi), Micro, Small & Medium Enterprises MSME-Development Institute. Retrieved from http://dcmsme.gov.in/dips/Distt.%20Industrial%20Profile%20of%20Bhadohi.pdf accessed on 10 Mar 2017.

Alessie, R., Van, R., & Lusardi, A., (2011). Financial Literacy and Retirement Preparation in the Netherlands, *Journal of Pension Economics and Finance, 10*(4), 527-545. doi: https://doi.org/10.1017/S1474747211000461

Aragaw, Y. (2011). Rural Micro Financing and Women's Empowerment: A Case Study on Rural Women Clients in Dessie Zuria District, Ethiopia, *International Journal of Rural*

Development and Management Studies, 5(1), 115-144. Retrieved from *www.serialsjournals.com/serialjournalmanager/pdf/1331795354.pdf*

Arora, S., & Bhandari, U.S. (1999). Socio-Economic Conditions of Tribals in Andhra Pradesh, New Delhi: *Institute of Applied Manpower Research*, 78.

Aruna, M., & Rema, J. (2011). The Role of Microfinance in Women Empowerment- A Study on the SHG Bank Linkage Program in Hyderabad (ANDHRA PRADESH), *Indian Journal of Commerce and Management Studies*, *2*(4), 77-95. Retrieved from https://www.microfinancegateway.org/library/role-microfinance-womens-empowerment-study-shg-bank-linkage-program-hyderabad-andhra-pradesh

Ayadurai, S. (2004). An Insight Into the Constraints Faced by Women Entrepreneurs in a War-Torn Area: Case Study of the Northeast of Sri Lanka, Paper presented at the 50th World Conference of the International Council for Small Business (ICSB), Washington.

Baluja, G. (2016). Financial Literacy among Women in India: A Review, *Pacific Business Review International, 9*(4), 82-88. Retrieved from http://www.pbr.co.in/October2016/11.pdf accessed on 15 Sept 2017.

Barat G.C., & Sandip, K.B. (2011). Micro Sector – Present Need, *International Journal of Marketing and Human Resource Development, 1*(1-2), 11-20.

Bhardwaj, G.N., Parashar, S., Pandey, B., & Sahu, P. (n.d.). Women Entrepreneurship in India: Opportunities and Challenges. Research paper. Retrieved from *https://chimc.in/admin/files/Gurendra%20Nath%20Bhardwajpdf.pdf*

Baro, P.K., & Sarania, R. (2014). Employment and Educational Status: Challenges of Women Empowerment in India, *Pratidhwani the Echo, 2*(4), 55-63. Retrieved From http://www.academia.edu/6919456/Employment_and_Educational_Status_Challenges_of_Women_Empowerment_in_India accessed on 12 Apr 2017.

Basu, S. (2005). White Paper: Financial Literacy and the Life Cycle. White House Conference on Aging. Available from: http://216.87.66.5/member /govt_relation.

Bathliwala, S. (1995). Defining Women's Empowerment: A Conceptual Framework. Education for Women's Empowerment, ASPBAE Position Paper for the Fourth World Conference on Women, Beijing, New Delhi, Asia-South Pacific Bureau of Adult, Retrieved from and accessed on http://www.hup.harvard.edu/catalog/SENPOP.html accessed on 19 Feb 2017.

Bhatt, M.A. (2015). Problems against the Tribal Women Entrepreneurs in Cottage Industries, *International Multidisciplinary Research Journal, 2*(8), 1-4.

Bhatt, E. (2006). We Are Poor But So Many: The Story of Self-Employed in India. New Delhi: *Oxford University Press*.

Bhattacharya, R. (2015). Ushering Gender Equality: Deutsche Bank India Raises Top Management Diversity to 40 per cent Women, *The Economic Times*, 8th Aug. 2015, p.5. Retrieved from https://economictimes.indiatimes.com/articleshow/48398497.cms?utm_source=contentofinterest&utm_medium=text&utm_campaign=cppst accessed on 15 Sept 2017.

Bhowmik, S.K. (2000). Hawkers in the Urban Informal Sector: A Study of Street Vendors in Six Cities, National Alliance of Street Vendors of India. www.nasvinet.org.

Bhowmik, S.K. (2005). Street Vendors in Asia: A Review, *Economic and Political Weekly, 40*(22-23), 2256-2264. Retrieved from https://www.epw.in/journal/2005/22-23/review-labour-review-issues-specials/street-vendors-asia-review.html

Bhowmik, S.K. (2007). Street Vending in Urban India: The Struggle for Recognition, In C.C. John and A. Morales eds. Street Entrepreneurs: People, Place and Politics in Local and Global Perspective. New York: Routledge.

Biswal, K.C. (2013). Tribal Entrepreneurship: A Study of Megahalaya State, In R.C. Miryala, ed., Changing Paradigms of Rural Management. New Delhi: *Zenon Academic Publishing*.

Blackman, A.J. (2003). Entrepreneurs Inter Relationship between Characteristics, Values, Expectations, Management Practice and SME Performance, School of Business Department of Management, Griffith University, Gold Coast Campus.

Bogaert, M.V.D., Toppa, E., & Das, N.C. (1972). Tribal Entrepreneurs, *ICSSR Research Abstracts Quartely, 11*(4), 250-264.

Bogaert, S.L. etal. (1975). Developing Entrepreneurs and Entrepreneurship in Typical Backward or Primitive Areas: A Case Study of the Ranchi District in Chhotanagpur, Seminar on Entrepreneurship. New Delhi, 54-61.

Boruah, R., Borua, S., Deka, C.R., & Borah, D. (2015). Entrepreneurial Behaviour of Tribal Winter Vegetable Growers in Jorhat District of Assam, *Indian Research Journal of Extension Education, 15*(1), 65-69. Retrieved from https://www.seea.org.in/vol15-1-2015/13.pdf

Bosma, N., & Harding, R. (2006). Global entrepreneurship monitor: GEM 2006 summary results. Babson Park, MA: Babson College, London, UK, London Business School. Retrieved from http://entreprenorskapsforum.se/wp-content/uploads/2010/02/GEM-Global-Report_2006.pdf accessed on 15 Sept 2017.

Bowen, N., & Guo, S. (2011). Structural Equation Modeling. New York: *Oxford University Press*. ISBN: 9780195367621

Browne, M., & Cudeck, R. (1993). Alternative Ways of Assessing Model Fit. *Sage Focus Edition*, 154, 136. ISBN: 9780803945074

Budlender (2011). Measuring Informal Employment in South Africa, The New Quarterly Labour Force Survey. *WEIGO Statistical Brief No. 7*. Retrieved from www.inclusivecities.org/wp-content/uploads/2012/07/Budlender_WIEGO_SB7.pdf

Bulsara, H.P., & Vaidehi, P. (n.d.). Developing Women Entrepreneutrship: A Challenge, In Entrepreneurship: Issues and Challenges Anthology, *Allied Publications*, 387-406.

Carmnines, E.G., & Mclver, C.J. (1981). Analyzing Models with Unobserved Variables: Analysis of Covariance Structures. In Bohrnstedt, G.W. & Borgatta, E.F. [Eds.] Social Measurement: current issues, Beverly Hills: *Sage*. ISBN 978-0803915961, doi: 10.117/004912418301 1003003

Carr, M., & Chen, M. (2004). Globalisation, Social Exclusion and Work with Special Reference to Informal Employment and Gender. Policy Integration Department Working Paper No. 20, Geneva: International Labor Office.

Chay, Y.W. (1993). Social support, Individual Differences, and Well-being: A Study of Small business Entrepreneurs and Employees, *Journal of Occupational and Organizational Psychology, 66*(4), 285-302. doi: http://dx.doi.org/10.1111/j.2044-8325.1993.tb00540.x

Choudary, K.V.R. (1981). Entrepreneurial Activity in North East Region: An Overview, *SEDME Journal, 8*(1), 35-44.

Cheung, W., & Rensvold, R. (2002). Evaluating Goodness-of-fit Indexes for Testing Measurement Invariance, *Structural Equation Modeling, 9*(2), 233-255, doi: http://dx.doi.org/10.1207/S15328007SEM0902 5

Chung, B., Kantachote, K., Mallick, A., Polster, R., & Roets, K. (2013). Indicators of Women' s Empowerment in Developing Nations By. Robert M.La Follette School of Public Affairs, University of Wisconsin-Madison, 1-95, La Follette School of Public Affairs, 1225 Observatory Drive, Madison, WI 53706 Retrieved from https://www.lafollette.wisc.edu/images/publications/workshops/2013-women.pdf accessed on 12 Apr 2017.

Cohen, M. (2000). Women Street Vendors: The Road to Recognition, *SEED Publication No. 20*.

Cohen, M., & Tinker, I. (1985). Street Foods: Opportunities for Female Employment in the Food System [horizon.documentation.ird.fr/exl-doc/pleins-textes/pleins-textes-4/colloques/17971.pdf.].

Cohen, M., Bhatt, M., & Horn, P. (2000). Women Street Vendors: The Road to Recognition. Working Paper SEEDS Paper No. 1 New York: Population. Council eprints.lse. ac. ukl ... /Urban labour market changes and social protection for urban informal workers challenges for China and India

Companion, M. (2007). Adaptability and Survival: A Case Study of Street Vendor Responses to Famine Conditions in Ethiopia 1999, In C.C. John and A. Morales eds. Op cit., 223-44.

Covin, J.G. (1991). Entrepreneurial Versus Conservative Firms: A Comparison of Strategies and Performance, *Journal of Management Studies, 28*(5), 439–462. Retrieved from http://

onlinelibrary.wiley.com/doi/10.1111/j.1467-6486.1991.tb00763.x/ abstract accessed on 08 Aug 2017.

Cross & Karides (2007). Capitalism, Modernity and Appropriate Use of Space, In C.C. John and A. Morales, eds. Op. cit., 19-25.

Cross, J., & Morales, A. (2007). Street Entrepreneurs: People, Place and Politics in Local and Global Perspective. London: Routledge.

Dandhi, K.L., & Intodia, S.L. (2001). Entrepreneurship: A Way to Employment Generation among Tribal and Non-Tribal Educated Rural Youth in Southern Rajasthan, *Journal of Indian Education, 26*(4).

Das, M. (1999). Women Entrepreneurs from Southern India: An Exploratory Study, *The Journal of Entrepreneurship, 8*(2), 147-163. https://doi.org/10.1177/097135579900800202

Dashora, R., & Sharma, A. (2003). Tribal Women Entrepreneurs, Social Welfare, 50(2), 15-24.

Datta, K. (2015). Women@ work Can be Unequal Battle, Kanika Datta: Life without Air India, *Business Standard*, 19 Nov 2015, p.9. Retrieved from http://www.businessstandard.com/article/opinion/kanika-datta-life-without-air-india-115111901300_1.html accessed on 10th Aug 17.

Deb, A.K. (2015). Micro Entrepreneurship for Women Self Reliance: A Study in Tripura, *International Journal of Economic and Business Review, 3*(2), 234-37.

Drexler, A., Fischer, G., & Schoar, A. (2014). Keeping It Simple: Financial Literacy and Rules of Thumb, *American Economic Journal: Applied Economics, 6*(2), 1-31. doi: https://doi.org/10.1257/app.6.2.1

Dixit, A., & Pandey, A. (2010). Entrepreneurship and Marketing among Tharu Tribe in India, *Journal of Global Economy, 6*(2), 117-36. Available at SSRN: https://ssrn.com/abstract=1620883

Edwards, G. (2007). The Role of Banks in Economic Development, *Macmillan*, London, (2004), "ENSR", The European Observatory for SMEs.

Eleventh Five Year Plan (2007-12), Retrieved from Planning Commission.nic.in/p1ans/planrel/11thf.htm

Gill, O. (1990). How to Understand Financial Statements: Get to Grips with Profit and Loss Accounts, Balance Sheets and Business Ratios, *Crisp Publications Inc*.

Government of India (2012). Report of the Committee on Unorganised Sector Studies.

Gundry, L., & Welsch, H. (2001). The Ambitious Entrepreneur: High Growth Strategies of Women-Owned Enterprises, *Journal of Business Venturing, 16*(5), 453-470, doi: https://doi.org/10.1016/S0883-9026(99)00059-2

Gundry, L., Kickul, J., Welsch, H. P., & Posig, M. (2003). Technological Innovation in Women-Owned Firms: Influence of Entrepreneurial Motivation and Strategic Intention, *The International Journal of Entrepreneurship and Innovation, 4*(4), 265-274, doi: https://doi.org/10.5367/000000003129574324

Hair, J., Black, W., Babin, B. & Anderson, R. (2010). Multivariate Data Analysis, New Jersey: Prentice-Hall. ISBN: 9780138132637

Hajong, D., & Sharama, J.P. (2010). Socio Psychological Correlates of Tribal Entrepreneurship Development, *Indian Research Journal of Extension Education, 10*(3), 27-31. Retrieved from http://seea.org.in/ojs/index.php/irjee/article/view/603

Hazarira, B.S. (2013). Problems and Prospects of Women Entrepreneurship in Sonowal Kachari Society, *Journal of Humanities and Social Science, 1*(4), 143-151. Retrieved from http://journaldatabase.info/articles/problems_prospects_ women.html

Heibrunn, S. (2008). Factors Influencing Entrepreneurial Intensity in Communities, *Journal of Enterprising Communities: People and Places in the Global Economy, 2*(1), 37 - 51, doi: 10.1108/17506200810861249.

Herrera, J., Kuepie, M., Nordman, C., Oudin, X., & Roubaud, F. (2012). Informal Sector and Informal Employment: Overview of Data for 11 Cities in 10 Developing Countries, Women in Informal Employment: Globalizing Organizing (WIEGO). Working paper No.9, January.

Hilgert, M.A., Hogarth, J.M., & Beverly, S.G. (2003). Household Financial Management: The Connection Between Knowledge and Behaviour, *Federal Reserve Bulletin, 89* (July), 309-322. Washinton, D.C. Retrieved from https://econpapers.repec.org/article/fipfedgrb/y_3a2003_3ai_3ajul_3ap_3a309-322_3an_3av.89no.7.htm

Honig, B. (1998). What Determines Success? Examining the Human, Financial, and Social Capital of Jamaican Micro-entrepreneurs, *Journal of Business Venturing, 13*(5), 371-394. doi: https://doi.org/10.1016/S0883-9026(97)00036-0

Hu, T., & Bentler, P. (1999). Cutoff Criteria for Fit Indexes in Covariance Structure Analysis: Conventional Criteria Versus New Alternatives, *Structural Equation Modeling: a Multidisciplinary Journal, 6*(1), 1-55, doi: http://dx.doi.org/10.1080/10705519909540118

Hugon, P., & Farrugia, C. (1989). The Informal Sector: Women and Development Planning. Africa. Analytical and Methodological Studies of the Division of Studies for Development. FEM.3. *UNESCO Publication*.

ILO (2010). Rural Women's Entrepreneurship Is "Good Business!" Gender and Rural Employment. Policy Brief #3.

International Labour Organisation Office (2002). Women and Men in the Informal Sector: A Statistical Picture. Geneva: International Labour Organisation Office.

Irene, R., Charles, L., & Japhet, K. (2015). Effects of Microfinance Services on the Performance of Small and Medium Enterprises in Kenya, *African Journal of Business Management, 9*(5), 206-211. doi: http://dx.doi.org/10.5897/AJBM2014.7519.

Jagirdar, M.P. (1986). Sericulture for Tribal Women, National Conference on Tribal Women and Development - Problems and Perspectives. Udaipur, July 30.

Francesca, A., & Moller, J. (2003). Cambodia Women Micro Entrepreneurs and their Business Needs. Urban Research Group. November (Draft Report).

Jutting, J.P., & Laiglesia, J.R. (2009). Employment, Poverty Reduction and Development: What's New? Jutting and J.R. Laiglesia, eds. Is This Informal Normal? Towards More and Better Jobs in Developing Countries. J.P. Paris: OECD.

Kabeer, N. (2001). Conflicts over Credit: Reevaluating the Empowerment Potential of Loans to Women in Rural Bangladesh, *World Development, 29*(1), 63-84. doi: https://doi.org/10.1016/S0305-750X(00)00081-4

Kabeer, N. (2001). Reflection on the Measurement of Women's Empowerment-Theory and Practice, In Discussing Women's Empowerment- Theory and Practice. Stockholm.

Kalyani ,W., & Chandralekha, K. (2000). Association between Socio-economic Demographic Profile and Involvement of Women Entrepreneurs in Their Enterprise Management, *Journal of Entrepreneurship, 11*(2), 219-248.

Kaur, R., & Bawa, S. (1999). Psychological Correlates of Entrepreneurial Performance among Women, *Journal of Entrepreneurship, 8*(2), 195-205. doi: *journals.sagepub.com/doi/pdf/10.1177/097135579900800204*

Kefela, G.T. (2010). Promoting Access to Finance by Empowering Consumers – Financial Literacy in Developing Countries, *Education Research Reviews, 5*(5), 205 – 212. Retrieved from http://www.academicjournals.org/article/article1379607640_kefela.pdf accessed on 18 Sept 2017.

Khanka, S.S. (2001). Entrepreneurial Development. New Delhi: *S. Chand and Co.*

Khanka, S.S., & Bisht, N.S. (1987). Opportunity Conditions Influencing Entrepreneurship in the Kumaun Hills (U.P), *Indian Psychological Abstracts, 27*(2), 199-200.

Kiggundu, M.N. (2002). Entrepreneurs and Entrepreneurship in Africa: What is Known and What Needs to Be Done, *Journal of Development Entrepreneurship, 7*(3), 239-258. Retrieved from https://www.researchgate.net/publication/291786374_Entrepreneurs_and_entrepreneurship_in_Africa_What_is_known_and_what_needs_to_be_done

Kinyua, R.W. (2012). A Survey of Relationship between Entrepreneurship Training and Self-Employment: Adventure of Gikomba Market Business Enterprises, unpublished MBA thesis, Kenya Methodist University.

Krejcie, R.V., & Morgan, D.W. (1970). Determine Sample Size for Research Activities, *Educational and Psychological Measurement, 30*(3), 607-610. doi: https://doi.org/10.1177/001316447003000308

Kumar, S.A. (2008). Small Business and Entrepreneurship. N.p.: I. K. International.

Kumar, S. (2012). Promoting Entrepreneurship in a Tribal Region: A Case Study of Mandar Block (Ranchi District), *Anusandhanika, 4*(2), 152-57. Retrieved from https://search.proquest.com/openview/d7afa830ff2385a2c9c4439f6893a294/1?pq-origsite=gscholar

Kumar, S., & Anees, M. (2013). Financial Literacy & Education: Present Scenario in India, *International Journal of Engineering and Management Research, 3*(6), 83-87. Retrieved from http://www.ijemr.net/december2013issue/financialliteracy&education-presentscenarioinindia%2883-87%29.pdf accessed on 08 Sept. 2017.

Kurbah, S. (2013). Role of Women Entrepreneurs in the Economic Development of Meghalaya: A North Eastern State, India, *International Journal of Engineering Business and Enterprise Applications (IJEBEA), 13*, 175 -185. Retrieved from iasir.net/IJEBEApapers/IJEBEA13-156.pdf

Kyoko, K. (2003). Market and Gender Relations: A Case of Women Retail Traders in Phnom Penh, *International Feminist Journal of Politics, 5*(1), 10. Retrieved from http://www.academia.edu/2413104 Market_Class_and_Gender_Relations_A_Case_of_Women_ Retail_Traders_in_Phnom_Penh

Lacity, M., & Jansen, M.A. (1994). Understanding Qualitative Data: A Framework of Text Analysis Methods, *Journal of Management Information System, 11*(2), 137-155. Retrieved from http://www.jstor.org/stable/40398109 accessed on 25 Oct 2017.

Lalhunthara (2015). Entrepreneurship and Gender: A Case Study of Micro Enterprises in Aizawl District, Mizoram, *International Journal of Business and Management, 3*(8), 46-51.

Lalrinawma, V.S. (2005). Mizo Ethos; Changes and Challenges. Aizawl: *Mizoram Publication Board*.

Langowitz, N., & Minnit, M. (2007). The Entrepreneurial Propensity of Women, *Entrepreneurship Theory and Practice, 31*(3), 341-364, doi: 10.1111/j.1540-6520.2007.00177.x

Lechner, C., Dowling, M., & Welpe, I. (2006). Firm Networks and Firm Development: The Role of the Relational Mix, *Journal of Business Venturing, 21*(4), 514"540. doi: https://doi.org/10.1016/j.jbusvent.2005.02.004

Lee, J. (1996). The motivation of Women Entrepreneurs in Singapore, *Women in Management Review, 11*(2), 18-29. doi: https://doi.org/10.1108/09649429610112574

Low, M.B., & Macmillan, I.C. (1988). Entrepreneurship: Past Research and Future Challenges, *Journal o f Management, 14*(2), 139-161, doi: https://doi.org/10.1177/014920638801400202

Lusardi, A. (2004). Saving and the Effectiveness of Financial Education. Pension Research Council WP2003-14. Available at SSRN: https://ssrn.com/abstract=476022 or http://dx.doi.org/10.2139/ssrn.476022

Lusardi, A., & Mitchell, O.S. (2007). Financial Literacy and Retirement Preparedness: Evidence and Implications for Financial Education Programs. Michigan Retirement Research Center Research Paper No. WP 2006-144. Available at SSRN: https://ssrn.com/abstract=957796 or http://dx.doi.org/10.2139/ssrn.957796

Lusch, R.F., & Laczniak, G.R. (1989). Macroenvironmental Forces, Marketing Strategy and Business Performance: A Futures Research Approach, *Journal of the Academy of Marketing Science, 17*(4), 283-295. doi: https://doi.org/10.1007/BF02726639

Lyon, F. (2007). Institutional Perspectives on Understanding Street Retailer Behaviour and Networks: Cases from Ghana. In C.C. John and A. Morales eds. Op.cit.

Malhotra, A., Schuler, S.R., & Boender, C. (2002). Measuring Women's Empowerment as a Variable in International Development. World Bank, Washington, D.C.

Mali, D. (1989). Development of Tribal Entrepreneurship in NER, *Journal of NEC*. Jan-March.

Mandell, L. (2008). Financial Literacy of High School Students. In: Xiao J.J. (eds) Handbook of Consumer Finance Research, *Springer*, New York, NY. doi: https://doi.org/10.1007/978-0-387-75734-6_10

Manimekalai, N. (2004). Impact of Various Forms of Micro Financing of Women. Ministry of HRD, India.

Masood, T., & Ahmad, I. (2009). An Econometric Analysis of Inter-State Variations in Women's Labour Force Participation in India. Munich Personal RePEc Archive, (47061) Retrieved from https://mpra.ub.uni-muenchen.de/19376/1/MPRA_paper_19376.pdf accessed on 19 Feb 2017.

McClelland, D. (1961). The Achieving Society. Princeton, NJ: N.P *D. Van Nostrand*.

McCrae, R.R., & Costa, P.T. (1987). Validation of the Five Factor Model of Personality Across Instruments and Observers, *Journal of Personality and Society Psychology, 52*(1), 81-90. doi: https://www.ncbi.nlm.nih.gov/pubmed/3820081

Mehrotra, S., & Biggeri, M. (2007). Social Protection in the Informal Economy: Home Based Women Workers and Outsourced Manufacturing in Asia. Working paper No. 97. Florence *UNICEF Innocenti Research Unit*.

Migiro, S.O. (2005). Small and Medium Scale Manufacturing Enterprises in Kenya: A Perspective on Alternative Sources of Financing. Retrieved from http://hdl.handle.net/10530/1170 accessed on 17 Jun 2017.

Millennium Development Goals, www.un.org/millenniumgoals.

Mishra, S.P. (1996). Factors Affecting Women Entrepreneurship in Small and Cottage Industries in India. International Labour Organisation, Swedish International Development Cooperation Agency

Mishra, B.R. (2015). Now, A Venture Fund for Women Entrepreneurs, *Business Standard*, 14th Sept 2015, p.10. Retrieved from http://www.business-standard.com/article/companies/now-a-venturefund-for-women-entrepreneurs-115091400024_1.html accessed on 05 Aug 2017.

Mishra, B.B., & Bal, K. (1997). Women Entrepreneurs in Orissa, A Study of Their Profile, Motivation and Constraints, *Indian Journal of Commerce, 1*, 193, part 4:385.

Mohapatra, A.S., Behera, R., & Sahu, U.N. (2012). Accessibility of Credit Facilities of Tribal Entrepreneurs of Mauyrbhanj District in Orissa, India, *International Journal of Research in Management, 1*(2), 101.

Mohapatra, A.S., Behera, R., & Sahu, U.N. (2012). Constraints Faced by Tribal Entrepreneurs in Dairy Farming Enterprise, *International Journal of Physical and Social Sciences, 2*(7), 171-84. Retrieved from http://www.indianjournals.com/ijor.aspx?target=ijor:ijpss&volume=2&issue=7&article=017

Mohiuddin, A. (2002). Micro Credit Interventions in Promoting Micro Enterprises, Phase –II, Research Report Series, 32, Hyderabad: NIRD.

Morris, M., & Sexton, L. (1996). The Concept of Entrepreneurial Intensity: Implications for Company Performance, *Journal of Business Research, 36*(1), 5-13, doi: https://doi.org/10.1016/0148-2963(95)00158-1

Moulik, T.N. (1975). The Entrepreneurial Model in Primitive Economics from Profit Making to Social Change, Seminar of Entrepreneurship, New Delhi, 54-61.

Mujumdar, N.A. (2008). Inclusive Growth - Development Perspectives in Indian Economy, Academic Foundation.

Mustafa, Z. (2013). Prospects and Challenges of Women Entrepreneurship: A Study of the Women Entrepreneurs of Jammu and Kashmir, *Abhinav Journal of Research in Commerce and Management, 2*(6), 78-91. Retrieved from http://prj.co.in/setup/business/paper171.pdf accessed on 11 Feb 2017.

Muthen, L., & Muthen, B. (1998). Mplus [Computer Software]. Los Angeles, CA. Retrieved from https://www.statmodel.com/ accessed on 19 Feb 2017.

Mushtaq, Z. (2012). Pull and Push Factors Making Woman an Entrepreneur. Retrieved from http://evoread.blogspot.com/2012/06/pull-and-push-factors-making-woman.html of Wed 20 Jun 2012.

National Sample Survey Organisation (2005). National Sample Survey 2005. New Delhi: *The Ministry of Statistics and Program Implementation, Coordination and Publication Division*.

Navajas, S., Schreiner, M. , M., Meyer, R.L., Gonzalez-Vegas, C., & Rodriguez-Meza, J. (2000). Micro Credit and the Poorest of the Poor: Theory and Evidence from Bolivia, World Development. 28(2), 333-346. doi: https://doi.org/10.1016/S0305-750X(99)00121-7

Nayak, P., & Mahanta, B. (2009). Women Empowerment in India, *SSRN Electronic Journal, 5*(2), 155183, doi: http://doi.org/10.2139/ssrn.1320071 accessed on 10 Mar 2017.

Nelasco, S. (2008). Factors Deciding Enterprising Capacity of Women, *Rai Management Journal, 5*(1), 109-115. Retrieved from http://web.usm.my/aamj/16.2.2011/AAMJ_16.2.4.pdf, accessed on 22 Dec 2016.

Neog, A.K. (1984). Entrepreneurship Development in Tribal Societies - Problems and Prospects, In Bordoloi, ed. Application of Science and Technology for Tribal Development. Assam: Tribal Research Institute.

Nishanthi, H.M. (2014). Analysis of Entrepreneurial Traits of the Small Business Owners in Sri Lanka, *International Journal of Scientific and Research Publications, 4*(10), 1-7.

Noritake, A. (2008). Negotiating Space and Gender: Female Street Entrepreneurs in Seoul, Intersections: Gender and Sexuality in Asia and the Pacific, 17. Retrieved from http://intersections.anu.edu.au/issue17/noritake.htm

Ochieng (2012). Executive Compensation and Firm Financial Performance: A Critical Literature Review, Independent study paper, PhD, University of Nairobi.

OECD (2005). Improving Financial Literacy: Analysis of Issues and Policies. Paris, France: *OECD Publications* accessed on 19 Aug 2017.

OECD (2013). Improving Financial Literacy: Analysis of Issues and Policies. Organization for Economic Co-operation and Development, Paris: *OECD Publications* accessed on 19 Aug 2017.

Orhan, M., & Scott, D. (2001). Why Women Enter into Entrepreneurship: An Exploratory Model, *Women in Management Review, 16*(5), 232-247. doi: https://doi.org/10.1108/09649420110395719

Oseifuah, E.K. (2010). Financial Literacy and Youth Entrepreneurship in South Africa, *African Journal of Economic and Management Studies, 1*(2), 164-182, retrieved from https://doi.org/10.1108/20400701011073473 accessed on 08 Sept 2017.

Osman, M.K. (2011). Service Quality, Customer Satisfaction and Loyalty: The Moderating Role of Gender, *Journal of Business Economics and Management, 12*(2), 278-300. doi: 10.3846/16111699.2011.573308

Ostgaard, T.A., & Birley, S. (1996). New Growth and Personal Networks, *Journal of Business Research, 36*(1), 37 – 50. doi: https://doi.org/10.1016/0148-2963(95)00161-1

Otoo, M., Fulton, J., Ibro, G., & Deboer, J. (2010). Women Entrepreneurship in West Africa: The Cowpea Food Sector in Niger and Ghana, *Journal of Developmental Entrepreneurship, 16*(1), 37-63. doi: https://doi.org/10.1142/S1084946711001732

Otunga, R.N., Grephas, O., & Muyia, F.N. (1998). Socio-Economic Background and Informal Sector Business Performance of Women Entrepreneurs in Eldoret.IDS Working 529: 1-19

Pandey, D.K., & De, H.K. (2015). Entrepreneurial Behavior of Tribal Fish Farmers in Tripura, North East India, *Indian Journal of Fisheries, 62*(1), 149-52.

Pandula, G. (2011). An Empirical Investigation of Small and Medium Enterprises' Access to Bank Finance: The Case of an Emerging Economy, Research paper, *ASBBS, 18*(1), 255-273.

Parihar, P., Kher, S.K., Nanda, R., & Singh, S.P. (2013). Study on Entrepreneurial Competencies of Women Entrepreneurs in Jammu District of Jammu and Kashmir State, *Economic Affairs, 55*(1), 49-56, Retrieved from http://www.indianjournals.com/ijor.aspx?target=ijor:eaj&volume=58&issue=1&article=007 accessed on 29 Nov 2016.

Parmeshwaram, K.P. (1975). Entrepreneurial Development for Small Scale Industries in a Backward State - An Experiment in Achievement Motivation Training, Seminar on Entrepreneurship. New Delhi: Development Commissioner Small Scale Industries, 175-80.

Parthasarathi, I. (2000). Entrepreneurship in Tribal Areas, In P.J.V. Rao, ed. Entrepreneurship and Economic Development, Kanishka. New Delhi, 171-85.

Parveen, S., & Leonhauser, I. (2004). Empowerment of Rural Women in Bangladesh: A Household Level Analysis. Conference on Rural Poverty Reduction through Research for Development and Transformation, (October). Retrieved from https://www.researchgate.net/publication/242079831_Empowerment_of_Rural_Women_in_Bangladesh_A_Household_Level_Analysis accessed on 19 Feb 2017.

Pitt, M., & Khandaker, S.R. (1996). Household and Intra-household Impacts of the Grameen Bank and Similar Targeted Credit Programs I Bangladesh. World Bank Discussion Papers, No. 320, Washington, D.C.

Planning Commission (2008). Report on the Success and Failure of Self help group in India-Impediments and Paradigm. Voluntary Operation in Community and Environment.

Prabat, K. (2015). Ericsson India Hiring Women for Traditionally Male-Dominated Functions, The Economic Times, 17 Aug 2015, p.6. Retrieved from https://economictimes.indiatimes.com/industry/telecom/ericsson-india-hiring-women-for-traditionally-male-dominatedfunctions/articleshow/48515829.cms accessed on 05 Sept 2017.

Pradhan, K.C. (2011). Empowerment of Rural Women through Self Help Groups: A Study of South Odissa. The Millennium Development Goals: The Indian Journey. N.P.: *Allied Publishers*.

Prahlad, C.K. (2009). The Fortune at the Bottom of Pyramid, Eradicating Poverty through Profits. N.P: *Wharton School Publishing*.

Puhazhendhi, V., & Badatya, K.C. (2002). SHG Bank Linkage Program for Rural Poor-An Impact Assessment. Mumbai, India: National Bank for Agriculture and Rural Development. Retrieved from services.iriskf.org/data/articles/Document 130122006100.4532129.pdf

Qaiz, S.A. (2000). Role of Dhaka City Corporation in Urban Food Security, Paper presented at the Regional Seminar on Feeding Asian Cities, November 27 - 30, 2000, Bangkok, Thailand.

Ramakrishna, G. (2010). Micro Finance in India - A Tool for Women Employment. N.P.: *Eastern Book Corporation*.

Ranjula, B.S., & Fan, Y.W. (2007). Does Micro Finance Empower Women? Evidence from Self help Groups in India. Working paper series, Department of Economics, Uppsala University, Sweden.

Rathiranee, Y., & Semasinghe, D.M. (2015). Factors Determining the Women Empowerment through Microfinance: An Empirical Study in Sri Lanka, *International Journal of Social, Behavioral, Educational, Economic and Management Engineering, 9*(5), 1595-1599. doi: https://doi.org/10.1999/1307-6892/10001391

Remund, D.L. (2010). Financial Literacy Explicated: The Case for a Clearer Definition in an Increasingly Complex Economy, *Journal of Consumer Affairs, 44*, 276–295. doi: https://doi.org/10.1111/j.1745-6606.2010.01169.x

Sachidanand (1968). Tribal Village in Bihar: A Study in Unity and Extension. Delhi: *Concept Publishing Company*.

Sarri, K., & Trihopoulou, A. (2005). Female Entrepreneurs' Personal Characteristics and Motivation: A Review of the Greek Situation, *Women in Management Review, 20*(1), 24-36. doi: https://doi.org/10.1108/09649420510579559

Sawyerr, O.O., McGee, J., & Peterson, M. (2003). Perceived Uncertainty and Firm Performance in SMEs: The Role of Personal Networking Activities, *International Small Business Journal, 21*(3), 269-290. Retrieved from http://journals.sagepub.com/doi/abs/10.1177/0266242603021300 2#articleCitationDownloadContainer accessed on 23 Sept 2017.

Saxena, M.K., Kukreti, B. R., & Gihar, S. (2004). Entrepreneurial Attitude of Tribal Youth and Role of Education in Enhancing Entrepreneurial Competencies Among Tribes, *Vanya Jati, 52*(2), 1-6.

Schayek, R. (2011). The Effect of Strategic Planning, Entrepreneurship, Human and Financial Resources and Market Orientation on Small Business Performance.

Scheepers, R., Hough, J., & Bloom, J. (2007). Entrepreneurial Intensity: A Study of Established Companies in South Africa, *South African Journal of Economic and Management Sciences, 10*(2), 238-255. doi: https://doi.org/10.4102/sajems.v10i2.585

Schollhammer, H., & Kwiloff, A.H. (1933). Entrepreneurship and Small Business Management, *John Wiley and Sons*, New York, 1-608. ISBN: 0894642359.

Schumpeter, J.A. (1949). The Theory of Economic Development. Cambridge, MA: *Harvard University Press*.

Sen, M., Rastogi, S., & Vanneman., R. (2006). Disempowered by Whom? Gender vs. Generation in Family Decision Making. IHDS, (2), Retrieved from http://paa2006.princeton.edu/papers/61612 accessed on 19 Feb 2017.

Sethy, D.E. (1981). Developing Entrepreneurship among Tribals, *Indian Management, 20*(3), 36-41.

Setty, E.D. (2002). Field Approach to Developing Entrepreneurship in Rural and Tribal Communities. In C. Kondaiah, ed. Entrepreneurship in the New Millennium : Challenges and Prospects. New Delhi: *Tata McGraw-Hill*, 158– 69.

Shah, A. (2012). Business Strategies in the Emerging Markets, *Journal o f Asia-Pacific Business, 13*(1), 4-15. doi: http://dx.doi.org/10.1080/10599231.2011.616143

Shah, F., & Mustafa, Z. (2014). Prospects of Women Entrepreneurship: A Study of the Women Entrepreneurs of Kashmir Valley, *Arth Prabandh: A Journal o f Economics and Management, 3*, 103-116. Retrieved from http://prj.co.in/setup/business/paper171.pdf accessed on 17 Dec 2016.

Sharma, S., Rao, P. K., & Sharma, R. (2013). Role of Women in Decision-Making Related to Farm: A Study of Jammu District of J&K State. *International Journal o f Scientific and Research Publications, 5*(1), 1-4 Retrieved from http://www.ijsrp.org/research-paper-1301/ijsrp-p1356.pdf accessed on 19 Feb 2017.

Shaver, G., & Scott, R. (1991). Person, Process, Choice: The Psychology of New Venture Creation, *Entrepreneurship Theory and Practice, 16*(2), 23-45. Retrieved from http://cemi.com.au/sites/all/publications/Shaver%20and%20Scott%201991.pdf accessed on 11 Mar 2017.

Shobana, N., & Junofy, A. (2009). Rural Women Empowerment through Self Help Group, Empowerment of Rural Women in India, *Kanishka Publishers,* New Delhi.

Singh, K.S. (1974). Development of Tribal Entrepreneurship: Perspectives on Tribal Development and Administration, Papers and Proceedings of the Workshop. *NICD*, Hyderabad, 18–20 April.

Singh, N. P. (1976). Whither Tribal Entrepreneurship through Rural Electrification, *Yojana, 20*(16), 25-27.

Singh, M. (2003). Tribal Women and Labour: Problems of Tribal Domestic Help in Delhi, *Women's Link, 9*(2), 20-25.

Sithole, F.S. (1995). Gender Research on Urbanisation Planning and Evaluation. Harare: Zimbabwe *Women's Resource Centre and Network*.

Small Business Council (2004). Small Businesses in the Informal Economy: Making the Transition to the Formal Economy. London: Victoria Street.

Smith, L.C., & Byron, E. (2005). Is Greater Decision Making Power of Women Associated with Reduced Gender Discrimination in South Asia? *Food Consumption and Nutrition Division of the International Food Policy Research Institute*, (August) Retrieved from http://www.ifpri.org/publication/greater-decisionmaking-power-women-associated-reduced-gender-discriminationsouth-asia accessed on 12 Apr 2017.

Sabina, A., & Solava, I. (2007). Agency and Empowerment: A Proposal for Internationally Comparable Indicators, *Oxford Development Studies, 35*(4), 379-403. Available at SSRN: https://ssrn.com/abstract=2118589

Society for Elimination of Rural Poverty, www.serp.ap.gov.in

Solomon, B., & Tomb, D. (2013). The Important Role of Female Small Business Owners, *Economic Times*, Friday, 10 May. Retrieved from https://www.cnbc.com/id/100727457

Sorensen, J.B., & Chang, P.M.Y. (2006). Determinants of Successful Entrepreneurship: A Review of the Recent Literature. N.P.: MIT, Sloan School of Management.

Sorensen, J., & Patricia, C. (2006). Determinants of Successful Entrepreneurship: A Review of the Recent Literature. doi: http://dx.doi.org/10.2139/ssrn.1244663

Sreeramulu (2006). Empowerment of Women through Self Help Groups. N.P: Eastern Corporation,

Srinivas, S. (1995). Critical Samskriti of Tribal Development Programmes-A Case Study of Two Koya Villages, *Girijian Samskriti, 3*(1), 27-37.

Srivastav, N. & Syngkon, R. A. J. (2007). Marketing Management and Entrepreneurship Development in a Tribal Dominated Economy: A Case Study of Small Scale Industries in East Khasi Hills District of Meghalaya, *ICFAI Journal of Entrepreneurship Development, 4*(2), 28-47. doi: http://dx.doi.org/10.2139/ssrn.1817302

Srivastava, S., & Misra, R. (2017). Exploring Antecedents of Entrepreneurial Intentions of Young Women in India- A Multi-Method Analysis, *Journal o f Entrepreneurship in Emerging Economies, 9*(2), 181-206. doi: https://doi.org/10.1108/JEEE-04-2016-0012

Status of Microfinance in India (2014). National Bank for Agriculture and Rural Development, India.

Staudt, K. (2007). Street Vendors at the Border: from Political Spectacle to Bureaucratic Iron Cage? In C.C. John and A. Morales eds. Op. cit., 79-91.

Thaker, K., & Ahlwat, S. (2012). Entrepreneurial Interests and Training Needs of Tribal Farm Women of Amirgadh and Danta Talukas of Banaskanta District, Gujarat, *Indian Research Journal of Extension Education Special Issue, 1*, 296-302. Retrieved from http://seea.org.in/ojs/index.php/irjee/article/view/482/478

Thalavai, P.N., & Nadarajan, S. (2011). Impact of Micro Finance – An Empirical Study on the Attitude of Self Help Group Leaders in Kanya Kumari district – Tamil Nadu, *International Journal of Enterprise and Innovation Management Studies, 1*(3).

Thrikawala, S. (2011). Impact of Strategic Networks for the Success of SMEs in Sri Lanka, *World Journal of Social Sciences, 1*(2), 108 - 119. Available at SSRN: https://ssrn.com/abstract=2333280

UNDP (1993). Human Development Report. N.P. *Oxford University Press*.

UNDP (2013). Human Development Report. New York: n.p.

UNDP (1990, 1995, 2000, 2002, 2005 and 2007-08). Human Development Report. Retrieved from http://hdr.undp.org/en/global-reports and accessed on 10 Mar 2017.

UNFPA (2005). State of world population 2005, The Promise of Equality: Gender Equity, Reproductive Health and the Millennium Development Goals, *UNFPA*. Retrieved from http://www.unfpa.org/sites/default/files/pub-pdf/swp05_eng.pdf and accessed on 10 Mar 2017.

UNIDO (2001). Women Entrepreneurship Development in Selected African Countries. Working Paper No. 7.

United Nations Human Development Report (2013), Published for the United Nations Development Programme (UNDP). Retrieved from *hdr.undp.org/sites/default/files/reports/14/hdr2013_en_complete.pdf ISBN: 9789211263404*

Urban, B., & Sefalafala, M. (2015). The Influence of Entrepreneurial Intensity and Capabilities on Internationalization and Firm Performance, *South African Journal of Economic and Management Sciences, 18*(2), 260-276, doi: 10.17159/2222-3436/2015/v18n2a9

Varma, S. (2015). Girl Students Catch up, will soon Overtake boys in India, *The Sunday Times*, 24th Sept 2017, 1. Retrieved from https://timesofindia.indiatimes.com/toireporter/author-Subodh-Varma-479086803.cms accessed on 11th Oct. 2017.

Verma, P. (2015). Snapdeal Kicks off Diversity Initiatives Advitya' in a bid to attract and retain talent, *The Economic Times*, 4 Aug 2015, 8. Retrieved from https://economictimes.indiatimes.com/small-biz/startups/snapdeal-kicks-off-diversity-initiative-advitya-in-a-bid-to-attract-and- retaintalent/articleshow/48337273.cms accessed on 08 Jul 2017.

Völker-Albert, J. (2015). UBS/PwC Billionaire report reveals female billionaires outpace males. Retrieved from https://press.pwc.com/News-releases/ubs-pwc-billionaire-report-reveals-female-billionaires-outpace-males/s/5e206600-cb17-41b7-910d-545e7dcbfead accessed on 25 Oct 2017.

Vengotanakro, & Chozhule, K. (2006). Strengthening Market Linkages for Women Vegetable Vendors - Experiences from Kohima, Nagaland, India, Retrieved from https://toc.123doc.org/document/63961-strengthening-market-linkages-for-women-vegetable-vendors-experiences-from-kohima-nagaland-india.htm

Venkatesh, S.A. (2006). Off the Books: The Underground Economy of the Urban Poor. Cambridge, MA: *Harvard University Press*.

Verghese, G., & Thanzawna, R.L. (1997). A History of the Mizos. Volume –I, *Vikas Publishing House*, New Delhi. ISBN-13: 978-8125903079

Volkov, V. (2002). Violent Entrepreneurs: The Use of Force in the Making of Russian Capitalism. Ithaca, New York: *Cornell University Press*.

Wadhwa, P. (2015). Kiran Mazumdar Shaw is the sole Indian in self-made women billionaires list, *Business Standard*, 18 Mar 2017, 6. Retrieved from http://www.business-standard.com/article/current-affairs/kiran-mazumdar-shaw-is-the-sole-indian-in-self-made-women-billionaires-list-117030800598_1.html accessed on 15 Oct 2017.

Watson, J. (2007). Modeling the Relationship between Networking and Firm Performance, *Journal of Business Venturing, 22*(6), 852-874. doi: https://doi.org/10.1016/j.jbusvent.2006.08.001

Webb, J.W., Tihanyi, L., Ireland, R.D., & Sirmon, D.G. (2009). You Say Illegal, I Say Legitimate: Entrepreneurship in the Informal Economy, *Academy of Management Review, 34*(3), 492-510. doi: http://dx.doi.org/10.5465/AMR.2009.40632826.

Wijewardena, H., De Zoysa, A., Fonseka, T. & Perera, B. (2004). The Impact of Planning and Control Sophistication on Performance of Small and Medium-Sized Enterprises: Evidence from Sri Lanka, *Journal of Small Business Management, 42*(2), 209–217. doi: http://dx.doi.org/10.1111/j.1540-627X.2004.00106.x

Williams, C. (2004). Small Businesses in the Informal Economy: Making the Transition to the Formal Economy, *Small Business Service*. Available at SSRN: https://ssrn.com/abstract=2287001

William C.C. (2008). The Hidden Enterprise Culture: Entrepreneurship in the Underground Economy, *Growth and Change: A Journal of Urban and Regional Policy, 39*(4), 673-675. doi https://doi.org/10.1111/j.1468-2257.2008.00453.x

Williams, C.C., & Gurtoo, A. (2011). Evaluating Women Entrepreneurs in the Informal Sector: Some evidence from India, *Journal of Development Entrepreneurship, 16*(3), 351-65. doi: https://doi.org/10.1142/S1084946711001914

Williams, C.C., & Round, J. (2007). Entrepreneurship and the Informal Economy: A Study of Ukraines Hidden Enterprise Culture, *Journal of Developmental Entrepreneurship, 12*(1), 119–36. Available at SSRN: https://ssrn.com/abstract=2708402

Worthington, A.C. (2006). Debt as a Source of Financial Stress in Australian Households, *International Journal of Consumer Studies, 30*(1), 2–15. doi: https://doi.org/10.1111/j.1470-6431.2005.00420.x

World Economic Forum (2013). Global Gender Gap Report. Geneva. Retrieved from http://reports.weforum.org/global-gender-gap-report-2013/

World Bank (2001). Attacking Poverty. World Bank Report, *Oxford Press,* New York.

World Bank (2013). World Development Report 2013, *The World Bank*, Washington, DC. Retrieved from https://siteresources.worldbank.org/EXTNWDR2013/Resources/8258024-1320950747192/8260293-1322665883147/WDR_2013_Report.pdf and accessed on 10 Mar 2017.

Index

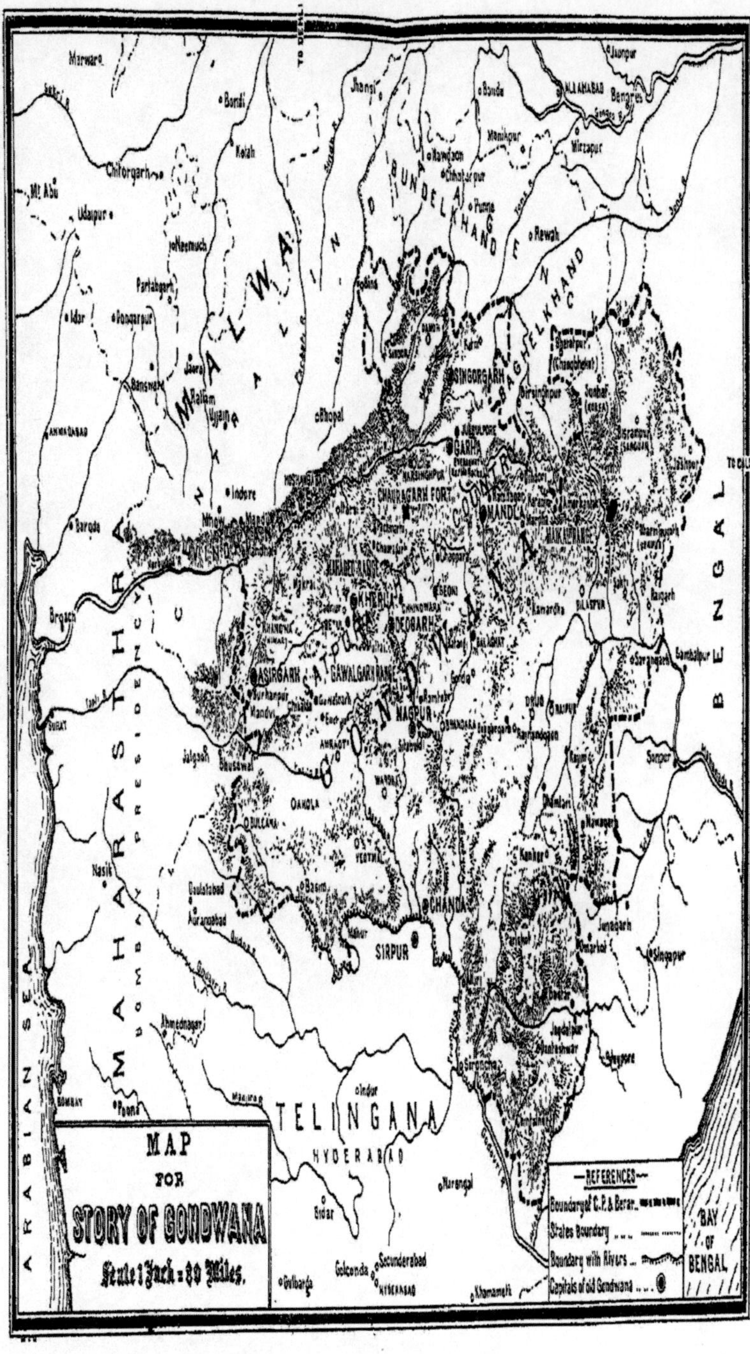
MAP
FOR
STORY OF GONDWANA
Scale 1 Inch = 80 Miles.
REFERENCES
Boundary of C.P. & Berar
States Boundary
Boundary with Rivers
Capitals of old Gondwana
ARABIAN SEA
BAY OF BENGAL
BENGAL
TELINGANA
HYDERABAD
MAHARASHTRA
BOMBAY PRESIDENCY
MALWA
BUNDELKHAND
BAGHELKHAND
GONDWANA
TO DELHI
TO CALCUTTA
Marwar
Bundi
Kotah
Jhansi
Banda
Allahabad
Benares
Jaunpur
Mirzapur
Manikpur
Chitorgarh
Mt. Abu
Udaipur
Neemuch
Partabgarh
Idar
Dungarpur
Banswara
Jaora
Ratlam
Ujjain
Bhopal
Indore
Mhow
Mandu
Baroda
Broach
Surat
Bombay
Poona
Ahmednagar
Aurangabad
Daulatabad
Nasik
Jalgaon
Bhusawal
Burhanpur
Asirgarh
Gawalgarh Range
Kherla
Deogarh
Nagpur
Chanda
Sirpur
Seoni
Balaghat
Garha
Jubbulpore
Singorgarh
Chauragarh Fort
Mandla
Maikal Range
Rewah
Panna
Chhatarpur
Bilaspur
Raipur
Drug
Sambalpur
Sarangarh
Raigarh
Jashpur
Sonpur
Kanker
Jagdalpur
Bastar
Sironcha
Junagarh
Singapur
Bidar
Golconda
Secunderabad
Gulbarga
Warangal
Khamamett
Akola
Buldana
Basim
Yeotmal
Amraoti
Bhandara
Damoh
Saugor
Sohagpur
Dhamtari
Nawagarh

INDEX

INDEX

INDEX

INDEX

INDEX

INDEX

THE END